Neolithic Flint Axes from the Cotswold Hills

Alan Tyler

British Archaeological Reports 25
1976

British Archaeological Reports
122 Banbury Road, Oxford OX2 7BP, England

GENERAL EDITORS

A.C.C. Brodribb, M.A.　　　　　　A.R. Hands, B.Sc., M.A., D.Phil.
Mrs. Y.M. Hands　　　　　　　　　D.R. Walker, B.A.

ADVISORY EDITORS

C.B. Burgess, M.A.　　　　　　　Neil Cossons, M.A., F.S.A., F.M.A.
Professor B.W. Cunliffe, M.A., Ph.D., F.S.A.
Sonia Chadwick Hawkes, B.A., M.A., F.S.A.
Professor G.D.B. Jones, M.A., D.Phil., F.S.A.
Frances Lynch, M.A., F.S.A.　　P.A. Mellars, M.A., Ph.D.
P.A. Rahtz, M.A., F.S.A.

B.A.R. 25, 1976: "Neolithic Flint Axes from the Cotswold Hills."
© Alan Tyler, 1976.

The author's moral rights under the 1988 UK Copyright,
Designs and Patents Act are hereby expressly asserted.

All rights reserved. No part of this work may be copied, reproduced, stored,
sold, distributed, scanned, saved in any form of digital format or transmitted
in any form digitally, without the written permission of the Publisher.

ISBN 9780904531282 paperback
ISBN 9781407318882 e-book
DOI https://doi.org/10.30861/9780904531282
A catalogue record for this book is available from the British Library

This book is available at www.barpublishing.com

NEOLITHIC FLINT AXES FROM THE COTSWOLD HILLS

CONTENTS

	Page
LIST OF FIGURES	
ACKNOWLEDGEMENTS	
INTRODUCTION	1
DISCUSSION	2
COMPLETE AXES	7
RE-USED FRAGMENTS	13
NOTES ON THE CATALOGUE	16
CATALOGUE	18
BIBLIOGRAPHY	86

**Please note that additional material is available to download from www.barpublishing.com/additional-downloads.html
The original foldouts have been reduced in size to match the A4 format of this book, the images are therefore not as clear as the original foldouts. Please refer to the original foldouts via the download for the original content.**

LIST OF FIGURES

		Page
1.	Clanfield, Oxon. (Cf) 1; Gloucester, (Gl) 3; Chippenham, Wilts. (Cp) 1.	90
2.	Crudwell, Wilts. (Cu) 2; Chalford, (Cd) 1; Stanton Harcourt, Oxon. (SH) 1.	91
3.	Gloucester, (Gl) 4; South Cerney, (SC) 1; Brockworth, (Bo) 1; Gloucester, (Gl) 2.	92
4.	Badgeworth, (Bd) 1; Stonehouse, (So) 2; Standlake, Oxon. (St) 1; North Nibley, (NN) 1.	93
5.	Cotswolds, (Cots) 1; Badgeworth, (Bd) 2; Stinchcombe, (Si) 1; Condicote, (Cc) 1; Aston Bampton, Oxon. (AB) 1.	94
6.	Barton-on-the-Heath, Warks. (BOH) 1; Gloucester, (Gl) 1; Lower Swell, (LS) 1; Wilson 3; Cassington, Oxon. (Cs) 2.	95
7.	Crudwell, Wilts. (Cu) 1; Cheltenham, (Ch) 1; Royce 1; Wilson 8.	96
8.	Map: Distribution of Complete Axes	97
9.	Map: Distribution of Axe Fragments	98

ACKNOWLEDGEMENTS

My thanks are due to all those people who have helped me during the preparation of this paper; to Professor R. J. C. Atkinson, Dr. J. G. Evans and Miss J. Price of University College, Cardiff; to the curators and staff of the various museums and private individuals, listed on page 17 of this paper, for their generous assistance in allowing me to study the material, for permission to publish specimens in their collections and for information about them; to Mr. B. Stallwood of the Archaeological Division of the Ordnance Survey; to Mr. R. Adkins of the Milton Keynes Development Corporation; to all those archaeologists and interested parties who answered queries, volunteered information and in various ways assisted me.

INTRODUCTION

The object of this paper is to compile a catalogue of all readily accessible information about the Neolithic flint axes of the Cotswolds, to note any evidence of production techniques, to show, where possible, that flint from broken axes was reused and to suggest possible parallels.

DISCUSSION

The area covered by this paper is somewhat larger than that defined by Buckman (1903, 206) or, more recently, by C. & A. M. Hadfield (1973, 15). The boundaries are set, where possible, on rivers, i.e. the Severn, Bristol Avon, Thames and Cherwell, while the northern one is an arbitrary line from Tewkesbury via Meon Hill and so to Fenny Compton which for part of the way follows the 400 foot (122 m) contour. The geology of the area is set out in detail in the various volumes of British Regional Geology (Kellaway & Welch, 1948; Sherlock, 1960; Edmunds & Oakley, 1958).

49 complete or almost complete Neolithic axes/adzes and some 468 fragments have been inspected or are known to exist from written or reliable verbal information. This does not include the material from the collection of the late Mr. E. A. Shore which is covered in a paper by Professor Tratman (1973). A breakdown of the total numbers gives:-

	Axes	%	Fragments	%
Flaked	10	20.4	9	1.9
Flaked & ground	3	6.1	-	-
Ground (including reflaked)	30	61.2	459	98.1
Unknown	6	12.2	-	-
	49	99.9	468	100.0

The known number of axes is in excess of this, as MF 10 has, for present purposes, only been counted as one, whereas the entry in VCH Wilts 1 (Grinsell, 1957, 90) mentions flint axes.

The material is principally in museum collections, which are derived, for the most part, from the private collections of persons with antiquarian interests, amassed in the late 19th/early 20th centuries and one very large private collection. They contain, for the most part, only the 'better pieces', complete artifacts or obvious fragments or flints of one particular type. This selectivity is further aggravated by the fact that one cannot recognise fragments of flaked axes unless they are large enough and obvious, usually the butt. Thus one has the rather absurd ratio of 98.1% ground fragments to only 1.9% flaked ones. Similarly only fragments of ground axes which include part of the outer surface are recognisable, which means that many fragments have to be passed over.

Distribution

The distribution pattern of axe fragments tends to fall into a series of groups but when this is compared with that of Neolithic field monuments, there is an almost total lack of agreement. Only on the high ground to the south of the River Frome, in the area covered by the Royce collection and at Ascott-under-Wychwood is there a similar pattern.

The distribution of axe fragments may represent nothing more than the areas of activity of their collectors but Bradley (1972/3, 200) has pointed out a similar lack of correlation between the find spots of stone axes and the distribution of long barrows in the Lake District and suggests that the axes were linked with the thinning of tree cover and the lopping of leaf-fodder well beyond the limits of domestic settlement. This inverse relationship between evidence for clearance and domestic settlement and number of axe finds has also been found in Wiltshire away from the Windmill Hill region. The areas of intensive land use, with long barrows and causewayed enclosures, where clearings would not easily regenerate contrasts strongly with rough browsing beyond, where grazing and sporadic gathering of winter fodder had less serious effects on tree cover.

The distribution of complete axes is different from that of either field monuments or fragments. It is predominantly lowland, 29 (59.1%) occurring below 400 feet (122 m). These may have been thickly forested areas in Neolithic times, the axes being used and lost in the forest, while the occurrence of four axes (AB 1, Bl 1, GR 1, So 2) in stream or river beds may have some significance of a ritual nature. It may be significant that the fragments which are known from below 400 feet (122 m) over O.D., (excepting material found during excavations) are large enough to be noticed casually and many of them are recorded as having been found during building operations/ditch digging or on spoil heaps as are complete axes from similar areas, i.e. only a selected part of the material is being recovered.

The nature of the soil is obviously a prime determinant in the distribution pattern. On the heavy clay soils of the valleys, the land is, for the most part, permanent pasture so there can be little surface flint collecting, while on the hills the soil is lighter and there is a tendency to arable farming, so collecting is possible. Soil depth also plays some part in the distribution pattern. People who collect flints in the area now all report concentrations of flints along slight ridges or along the uphill side of sloping fields, i.e. where the soil is thinner due to creep.

Another reason for the lack of collections from the long dip slope of the hills may be geographical. There are no large settlements on that part of the Cotswolds, hamlets and small villages occur only in the valleys along the spring lines. In small communities there was, in the past, less likelihood of a person sufficiently interested to assemble a collection.

Sources of Flint

Two main sources of supply of flint were available to early man, superficial deposits in the form of river gravels or nodules in surface soils, and deposits below the surface. The two nearest groups of flint mine sites to the Cotswolds are those at Durrington, Wilts., and Peppard Common, Oxon., although it must be remembered that stone axes were traded over long distances and ground or roughed out flint axes may have been brought from as far away as Norfolk.

However, there is another source of flint, in Gloucestershire, which one would expect to have been exploited in an area where the bulk of the flint used had to be imported. In the marly gravels at Moreton-in-Marsh, in the clay soils at Compton Scorpion and between Charingworth and Aston Magna, there are dark coloured and black flints which show no sign of having been affected by weathering, attrition or severe frost, some of which were reported to weigh 1 to 2 cwt. (50.8 to 101.6 kg) (Gray, 1912/3, 73). As to its source of origin there has been much speculation (Lucy, 1872, 71; Reade, Buckman & Callaway, 1903, 111; Gray, 1911, 260) and a final solution must await application of the trace element analysis techniques which have been recently developed (Sieveking et al., 1970, 251; Sieveking et al., 1972, 151) but it does need to be borne in mind when considering axe trade connections with other parts of the country. Again, it is reasonable to expect large lumps of flint from nearby riverine sources to have been used when available.

Exploitation of local sources of flint is further suggested by the large number of fragments of scrap flint with cortex adhering to them and the occasional lump of nodular flint e.g. that found near Frocester and now in the Witchell collection, which weighs about 2 kg. The alternative is that blocks of 'raw' nodular flint were traded from the mines to this area.

Manufacture of Axes

It is obvious that it was usual to flake off as much flint as possible before the grinding was started, because on occasion too much was removed, the residual flake scars bearing witness to this fact e.g. Kn 1, SC 1, Ce 36. This was almost certainly because of the length of time required for the grinding process. The medium used is unknown but to judge from the striae on some fragments, a coarse grinding powder, e.g. a silica sand, with a lot of water was usual. Alternatively the axes were ground on a block of sandstone, or some such material, as at Ehenside Tarn, Cumberland (Bunch & Fell, 1949, 14) and West Kennet (Piggott, 1962, 18). Cardew (1890/1, 249) noted that Mrs. Dent of Sudeley Castle had in her collection 'a hone worn into a deep trough by grinding axes' but unfortunately it has not been possible to trace it.

In almost every case where it is possible to see extensively striated areas on axes, the grinding was carried out parallel to the long axis of the axe for the sides, faces and flattened area where the body tapers to the edge. The edge edge quite often has fine striae which indicate grinding at right angles to the long axis or parallel to the edge but this may have been carried out subsequently during its period of use, e.g. Ar 3, Dw 1, Pr 40. While no axes appear to have been ground across their width, three have areas which show signs of having been ground at an angle of 45° to the long axis e.g. Gl 2, LN 13, Co 2. There may be more but one has difficulty recognising the symptoms on small fragments. Ce 4 has striae which suggests grinding in two directions, so it may be from a similar area of the axe. The most unusual striae are those on LN 95 which indicate that it has been ground with a circular motion.

None of the axes from the Cotswolds have the striae from the grinding process completely polished out. Axes or fragments which have polished areas are indicated in the corpus elsewhere in this paper. It is most likely that some of the polishing, particularly in the region of the edge, e.g. Bo 1, Gl 2, NN 1, derives from use, while Pr 22, Cotswolds 6, 7 & 9 have only one face polished in close proximity to the edge suggesting their use as adzes rather than as axes.

Another technique used was to grind only the edge and the area immediately behind it, leaving the rest of the axe in a flaked condition, e.g. Cc 1, AB 1, in order to produce a good cutting edge without the excessive production time needed for an axe which was totally ground.

What is not known is whether the flaked axes were intended to have been ground. Bruce Mitford (1938, 282) has argued that the market was flooded with serviceable flaked axes from mines opened up in the late Neolithic period which led to the demise of the ground axe. This will be considered below.

Hafting

None of the axes from the Cotswolds was recovered with any part of the haft in situ but a few of them bear some possible evidence of their hafts, or the position which they occupied. Smith (1965, 103) noted that the prevalence of transverse hinge fractures suggests that breakage occurred often at the point of entry into the haft; this is also borne out by fragments from the Cotswolds, e.g. So 1, Ka 2, Cotswolds 3 & 5, Royce 6, Co 11. One axe, Bd 1, and one fragment, LN 81, display fine striae which are unlike those usually produced during the grinding process. Bd 1 has a series of fine transverse scratches about the centre of gravity which may be the result of the axe moving in the haft during use. LN 81 is a polished face fragment but there are also fine scratches which may be either the result of the hafting, or the fine grinding medium used for the polishing. BOH 1 has been battered along the sides and to some extent across the faces and shows a distinct constriction where one would have expected the haft to have been. This again may have been caused during hafting, by movement of the head during use, or possibly created to provide a rough surface to enable glue to key onto the flint. How the chisels, e.g. Cs 2, were hafted is a matter for conjecture but study of the surface scratches as advocated by Semenov (1964, 126) may give a possible clue. It is also uncertain whether the small 'pear drop' axe, LS 1, was ever intended for use and if so, how it was mounted.

Weight

Weight variations in the axes tend to show three principal groups, around 150 g, around 225 g, and around 300 g, with the rest of the weights evenly distributed to 822 g (Cu 2). While these groups are in part due to the inclusion of badly damaged/worn axes, the variation no doubt reflects different functions but it may also be indicative of the progressive reclamation of axes/adzes as the larger ones were broken.

Faults and Blemishes

The reasons for breakages may be suggested in four instances amongst the axe fragments from the Cotswolds. Av 5 and Pr 21 both have a plug of siliceous material which passes right through the axe. As 12 has a 'vugh', a crystal lined void, which was probably inside the axe and not visible until fractured, while Ce 13 includes part of a fossil echinoid, Milcraster, and has fractured along the interface between fossil and flint. The sides of the fossil have been ground to the curvature of the face of the axe but an obvious crack shows in the flint. In three of these fragments the cause of the subsequent breakage could have been seen at the time of manufacture, suggesting that the persons who produced these axes were not unduly worried by surface cracks or blemishes, such as the 'vughs' which occur in the surface of Bd 1 and LN 12. This is further borne out by the occurrence on ground flint axes, not only from this area, of patches of cortex which have been left on and ground to shape.

Dating

No dates as such can be applied directly to any of these axes. The flakes from Ascot-under-Wychwood (except AUW 1) must be prior to the date of 2785 b.c. $\pm$ 70 (BM 492) obtained from charcoal on the old land surface. In the three cases where fragments of flint axes have been found in association with pottery in this area, Cam (Smith, 1968, 24), Cassington (Atkinson, 1947, 18) and Stanton Harcourt (Hamlin, 1963, 2; Case, 1963, 19) it is with late Neolithic or early Bronze Age wares, although Atkinson does make the point that the grave goods are of a period considered older than the tripartite urn. The parallels to Cs 2 with late Neolithic pottery (Manby, 1974, 90) and the evidence of the tools produced from the fragments, represent middle and late Neolithic traditions while the barbed-and-tanged arrowheads represent the Beaker/early Bronze Age tradition. These latter objects need not imply too much as an arrowhead can be made from fragments, already long discarded and picked up in a field.

Errata

The 'British hatchet of flint' excavated by Lysons (1821, 183) at Great Witcombe villa, now on loan to Cheltenham Art Gallery and Museum, and the ground axe from near Lechlade in the A. D. Passmore collection at the Ashmolean Museum (1955-120b), are of igneous rock, not flint.

The axe from Long Compton, Warks. (Clinch, 1904, 216; Bloxam,...., 12) is the same axe as that from Barton-on-the-Heath, Warks. (BOH 1).

Conclusions

Although flint axes do not appear to have been as plentiful in the Cotswolds as in comparable areas of Sussex and Wessex, it is obvious that they were not as scarce as has been thought in the past. It is impossible to estimate the numbers of complete axes that are represented, as it has been shown that flint from broken axes was reworked. The outward appearance of some of the axes shows similarities to others both in the Cotswolds and elsewhere but until systematic analysis of flint has been carried out on a scale comparable to that for the petrological identification of stone implements it would be unwise to suggest any origins for the axes. Similarly, until catalogues of flint axes are published for the whole of Britain any distribution patterns are likely to be false.

COMPLETE AXES

Details are given in the catalogue

Alveston (Al) 1

Found in the garden of a house in the village; ground; map reference of find spot but no other details known. In private hands in 1962. The O.S. Antiquities Catalogue (O.S. Ant. No. ST68 NW11) records that it was exhibited in a show and was described in a newspaper article 'Thornbury through the ages' between 1940 and 1950. This might be the same axe as Thornbury (Th) 1.

Badgeworth (Bd) 1   (Fig. 4)

Found immediately under the turf during the excavations at Crickley Hill (Dixon, 1972). No good parallels, though Mn 1 is similar, most likely due to extensive use and grinding. This has proceeded to the point where it interfered with the side of the axe. This side is flattened while the other is rounded, again suggesting much use.

Badgeworth (Bd) 2   (Fig. 5)

Found in the Neolithic bank during excavations at Crickley Hill (Dixon, 1972). Adze produced from a broken axe by reflaking the break for mounting in a knee-shaped haft. c.f. Si 1 and Cots 1. Edge apparently used and reground on one side prior to breakage, again suggesting change of use. The edge has an 'S' profile, which may indicate the form of the original axe. This is one of the few stratified pieces in this area.

Brockworth (Bo) 1   (Fig. 3)

There is no good parallel for this axe mainly due to its extensive use or misuse. Its side profile and section, however, have the same general shape as one from Stanton Downham, Sussex (Evans, 1897, 99).

Chalford (Cd) 1   (Fig. 2)

Found in the garden of a house; perhaps a recent import to the area but the patination and general appearance suggest that it was probably found locally. Similar axes have been found in the Thames at Kingston, Hampton Court, between Maidenhead Bridge and Boulters Lock, and Bray (Adkins, 1974, Nos. 88, 114, 111, 53) and Panshanger, Herts. (Cowper, 1863, 193). Larger axes of the same form include those from Cobham, Surrey (Harrison, 1968, 129), Botesdale, Suffolk (Evans, 1897, 111), and Crudwell, Wilts. (Cu 2). The butt of Cd 1 is damaged so that its original shape is unknown, but two butts, Cots 2 and Mn 2, may have come from similar axes. The edge has been removed by flaking, all the blows being from the one side and this same operation has given rise to the numerous small edge fragments which have been noted.

Chalford (Cd) 2

Whereabouts unknown.

Chedworth (Ct) 1

O.S. 1:10 000 sheet number SP01SW with the date 1916. Whereabouts unknown.

Chedworth (Ct) 2

Marked on the same map as Ct 1 with the find date of 1920, in the possession of a former vicar of the parish. Crawford (1925, 9, footnote) mentioned a "... polished flint axe from the parish which had never been examined by an archaeologist...." presumably one of these two; present whereabouts unknown.

Cheltenham (Ch) 1   (Fig. 7)

The colour change from light grey to dark grey is at right angles to the long axis and may have been deliberately arranged this way during the manufacture of the implement, or caused by the haft. There is no parallel for it in the Cotswolds and no obvious one from outside the area either, although the fragment Pr 28 which is made into a point may have come from an axe with a similar section.

Condicote (Cc) 1   (Fig. 5)

One of the few axes from the Cotswolds which has only the edge ground. There are similarities between this axe and those from Surbiton and Penton Hook (Adkins, 1974, Nos. 65, 12), both of which are smaller, from the chambered tomb at Ty Isaf, Brecknockshire (Grimes, 1939, 131) and from Burwell Fen, Cambs. (McKenny Hughes, 1897, 372).

Falfield (Fa) 1

This polished axe, found in the garden of a house, was presented to Bristol City Museum but could not be located.

Gloucester (Gl) 1   (Fig. 6)

This axe is labelled 'W. Gloucester' which could mean either the western part of the city or west of the city i.e. outside the area considered. The axe is similar to the fragment of a smaller axe from Newent, Glos. now in Gloucester City Museum (A 2993).

Gloucester (Gl) 2   (Fig. 3)

Found 'probably near Gloucester'; this appears to be a smaller and much battered version of St 1.

Gloucester (Gl) 3   (Fig. 1)

This and Gl 4 were both given the same place of origin but there is no evidence that they were found together. It is very similar to axes from Chippenham, Wilts. (Cp 1), Peaslake, Surrey (Bruce-Mitford, 1938, 281) and Ewhurst, Surrey (Lowther, 1957, 118), while Adkins (1974, No. 5) records an axe with a wider butt but otherwise of the same general shape.

Gloucester (Gl) 4   (Fig. 3)

Similar to SC 1. A slightly smaller axe from Kingston-on-Thames (Adkins, 1974, No. 91) bears comparison to these two, as does Ke 1, although in the latter case there is a sharper change between side and edge.

Lower Swell (LS) 1   (Fig. 6)

This may not be an axe but similar small pear-shaped objects occur on Neolithic sites (Smith, 1965, F117) (Wainwright & Longworth, 1971, F54) and for that reason it is included.

North Nibley (NN) 1   (Fig. 4)

Comparison can be made with axes from the Thames 'upstream of Magna Carta Island' and 'down-stream of Maidenhead Railway Bridge' (Adkins, 1974, Nos. 44, 54), the damaged axe So 2 and the edge fragment Mn 1. Perhaps a worn version of an axe similar to St 1.

South Cerney (SC) 1   (Fig. 3)

Similarities between this axe and Gl 4 have already been noted; the butt So 1 is also a good match. The edge has been reground at a much steeper angle than normal.

Stinchcombe (Si) 1   (Fig. 5)

The treatment of this piece is similar to that on Bd 2 and Cots 1.

Stonehouse (So) 2   (Fig. 4)

The curvature of the sides in plan, the side views and section are similar to NN 1, although the edge/side change is much sharper in the present case. A much worn and battered piece.

Thornbury (Th) 1

This may be the same axe as Al 1. Found during the digging of house foundations near Thornbury. Whereabouts unknown.

Uley (Ul) 1

This axe, and one of 'green stone', were in the Gordon Museum, Guy's Hospital, London; present whereabouts unknown.

Uley (Ul) 2

'Found in Uley long barrow in 1901' according to Accessions Card; on display but not accessible.

Royce 1   (Fig. 7)

This flaked adze is similar to a gouge from Westleton Walks, Suffolk (Evans, 1897, 179). The label states 'Cotswolds?' but it does not bear the characteristic patina of flint found in the area.

Aston Bampton, Oxon. (AB) 1   (Fig. 5)

Found in the Great Brook above Chimney; one form of a large number of finely made axes with concave sides, a ground edge and the rest of the axe flaked, which have been defined as 'Seamer' axes by Manby (1974, 98). Reflaked after grinding, as indicated by a small ground area remaining near the butt. Similar axes of this type are known from Teddington Lock and Teddington (Adkins, 1974, Nos. 28, 16) while Manby (1974, Fig. 40, Appendix 8) cites examples from the midlands and north of England. While axes of this form have a generally eastern distribution in Britain, examples are known from Wiltshire (Burchard, 1973, 118) and Cornwall (Needham, 1975).

Bloxham, Oxon. (Bl) 1

A polished axe described as 'chert', was reported to the Oxford City and County Museum but no records were made. Now in the possession of the finder near Grantham, Lincs.

Bruern, Oxon. (Bu) 1

Whereabouts unknown.

Cassington, Oxon. (Cs) 2   (Fig. 6)

A polished chisel found in dumped top-soil; no close parallels in the Cotswolds although a butt from Minster Lovell, Oxon. (ML 6) may be from such a chisel. Elsewhere in England, polished chisels are associated with late Neolithic material (Manby, 1974, 90) and with hoards of flint tools, as at Seamer Moor, Yorks. (Smith, 1920/1, 121) and Canewdon, Essex (Pollitt, 1931, 58).

Clanfield, Oxon. (Cf) 1   (Fig. 1)

Found while digging a land drain, it is similar to the axe from Witney, Oxon. (Wi 1). Similar axes occur in a hoard from Clayton Hill, Sussex (Curwen, 1929, 42), from Whitlingham, Norfolk (Smith, 1920/1, plate IV/2) and from Kingston, Surrey (Adkins, 1974, No. 7).

Grafton and Radcot, Oxon.   (GR) 1

Whereabouts unknown.

Great Tew, Oxon.   (GT) 1

Whereabouts unknown.

Kencot, Oxon. (Kn) 1

Resembles SC 1 and Gl 4 but the corner between side and edge is much more pronounced, an axe with a similar profile occurs in the Clayton Hill, Sussex, hoard (Curwen, 1929, 42).

Standlake, Oxon. (St) 1   (Fig. 4)

Similar axes are known from the Thames at Kingston and Bray Reach (Adkins, 1974, Nos. 93, 39) and from the Holkham, Norfolk, hoard (Smith, 1920/1, 113). The cutting edge of this axe has a shallow 'S' profile which may suggest that it was from an axe of this type that the adze Bd 2 originated.

Stanton Harcourt, Oxon. (SH) 1   (Fig. 2)

Similar to Cd 1 in plan but not in section. Another parallel comes from the Thames at Tilehurst (Adkins, 1974, No. 35).

Witney, Oxon. (Wi) 1

Paralleled by Cf 1. Whereabouts unknown.

Woodstock, Oxon. (Wo) 1

Whereabouts unknown.

Wilson 3   (Fig. 6)

This crude roughout has no obvious parallels. Most likely a reject, if indeed it was ever intended to be an implement. However some of the late Neolithic 'adzes' from Durrington Walls have a very rough appearance (Wainwright & Longworth, 1971, Fig. 22)

Wilson 8   (Fig. 7)

Appears to be a roughout and the above comments are applicable. F 86 from Durrington Walls (Wainwright & Longworth, 1971) may be part of a similar axe.

Charlcombe, Soms. (Co) 1

Whereabouts unknown.

Barton-on-the-Heath, Warks. (BOH) 1   (Fig. 6)

This axe type may have been common in the Cotswolds, as a number of fragments come from axes with a very pronounced surface curvature, i.e. As 18, Av 1, Cc 18, LN 1, 24 & 26, Pr 7 & 24, Sr 3, Ul 5, WUE 1. Similar axes occur in the hoards from Fleggburgh and Holkham, Norfolk (Smith, 1920/1, 113) and Bedham Hill, Sussex (Keef, 1940, 231).

Box, Wilts, (Bx) 8

Not located in Kingswood School Museum, Bath.

Chippenham, Wilts. (Cp) 1   (Fig. 1)

Very similar to Gl 3 and parallels are given under that heading.

Colerne, Wilts. (Cn) 1

Most of the B. H. Cunnington collection was given to Devizes Museum but this does not appear to have been amongst it.

Crudwell, Wilts. (Cu) 1   (Fig. 7)

Three axes Cu 1, 2 & 3 were found 'while digging the same drain', which suggests that they were not all found together. This axe and Cu 2 are the largest complete examples in this survey but there is some evidence that they were not unique. Cu 3 may have been of the same general size although this is not specifically stated. TG 1 is the edge fragment from an axe of similar size and the large core scraper Pr 20 must have been produced from an axe of similar dimensions. All five axes had been ground, while Cu 1 & 2 have a fine polished finish.

Crudwell, Wilts. (Cu) 2   (Fig. 2)

Parallels to this axe are given by Evans (1897, 111) while in this survey Cd 1 is similar though smaller.

Crudwell, Wilts.   (Cu) 3

Broken when found. Sent to Lady Cooper, who gave it 'to a collector'; present whereabouts unknown.

Monkton Farleigh, Wilts. (MF) 10

Axes formerly in a private collection believed to have been destroyed during the blitz on Bath 1941.

Monkton Farleigh, Wilts.   (MF) 26

Not located in Kingswood School Museum, Bath.

Cotswolds (Cots) 1   (Fig. 5)

This piece is similar to Bd 2 and Si 1.

RE-USED FRAGMENTS

This survey has revealed 62 obviously re-used fragments plus a further 27 which have secondary retouch on otherwise rough flakes. A breakdown of the re-used pieces follows:-

Scrapers	24	'Fabricators'	4
Arrowheads	6	Renewed Edges	4
Points	5	Adzes	3
Hammerstones	5	Grindstones	2
Cores	5	Discoidal Knife	1
Pot Boilers	4		

Adzes

Bd 2, Si 1 and Cots 1 were almost certainly axes, originally perhaps about 120 mm long, which broke giving a large fragment with a good edge. Re-use consisted of reflaking the break to a taper so that it could be hafted as an adze. All these are listed with the complete axes.

Renewed Edges

Similar recovery operations to put an edge on body fragments LN 12 and Pr 21, and butts Pr 3 and MF 6. On the first three the 'edge' has been achieved by flaking with no obvious attempt to produce a fine finish. Alternatively, these may be core scrapers which have fortuitously been produced from axe fragments. MF 6 on the other hand appears to be a small woodworking tool. The break has been ground at a steep angle to produce an edge, since destroyed.

Discoidal Knife

The subtriangular shape of Dw 1 suggests that it was used as a discoidal knife. The surface has been flaked over to achieve a slimmer profile but traces of striae from the original grinding remain, as does the good edge.

Grindstones

ML 4 is a body fragment which has a shallow groove parallel to what would be the long axis of the axe, if it were complete. This shows striae which run at a slightly different angle from those which result from the production of the axe. This area also carries a high polish, unlike the rest of the surface. There is no evidence that this was due to re-use of the broken axe but it is certainly secondary to the initial production and no woodworking technique is likely to cause such a depression. A similar shallow groove occurs on one face of Ke 1, extending from the break to the edge. If, as complete axes or adzes, they were intended to have had the fluting down the one face they are almost unique. It seems most likely that some unknown material, probably in rod form, was rubbed down on these fragments.

'Fabricators'

Bb 1 and Sr 5 are both corner fragments with severe abrasion at the broken ends, probably the result of use as 'strike-a-lights'. Another piece used both as a 'fabricator' and as a hammerstone was Br 1 (Clifford et al., 1954, 187). Royce 14 and Bx 7 are side fragments, the ends of which have had a few flakes removed. They thus have the characteristic section of 'fabricators' but Bx 7 shows no wear.

Points

Pr 28 is a side/face fragment retouched on the two ground faces to give a rough point/awl, the tip of which has since been lost. The group of points MF 11, 14, 15 & 16, are all of the same type and seem to be unique to the area. They have been produced from the edge of an axe and worked so that instead of a sharp point there is a small chisel end formed by the retention of a millimetre or so of the cutting edge. The retouch on them is predominantly on the one side of the flake and from the same face.

Scrapers

20 flake and 4 core scrapers are known. There are also 27 fragments with secondary retouch, probably used as scrapers. viz.

As 20: core	Pr 5: flake/core	Ul 17: rounded
As 22: pear shaped	Pr 14: end	Sa 2: rounded
Ce 1: rounded	Pr 20: core	Sa 4: rounded
Cc 3: rounded	Pr 23: rounded	Sa 5: rounded
Dy 2: rounded	Pr 29: rounded (possible)	SH 2: side
LN 54: rounded (possible)	Sr 1: end	Co 6: core (crude)
LN 78: rounded	Sr 6: oval	MF 22: end
Pr 22: rounded	Ul 4: rounded	Cotswolds 19: rounded

The various types of rounded flake scrapers have not been subdivided as the shape of the product is governed, to a large extent, by the starting material and is unlikely to be typical. The flake scrapers are all, with one exception, struck from the face of the axe, the resulting sharp edges then being retouched. In the cases MF 22 and Sr 1 the flakes are elongated and have been used as end scrapers, while Pr 14 is a large side fragment used for the same purpose. Fragment SH 2 was used to produce an irregular side scraper (Case, 1963, 19), while Pr 5 is so large that it could almost be classified as a core scraper, being a body fragment but for one face. The three already mentioned under 'renewed edges' and the small ovate LS 1 may also belong to this group.

Hammerstones

Five fragments show sufficient battering marks to justify this classification (Ar 1, Br 1, Pr 19, Sr 2, KA 1) but all the large body fragments show battered areas e.g. Pr 20.

Pot Boilers

Not tools except in the broadest sense, four fragments show the characteristic crazing and pitting associated with heating and rapid cooling (Ce 42, He 2, Sr 3, ML 1). However, there are other fragments which have been heated and may be the residue from the final destruction of such pieces.

Reflaked Axes

The reflaking of the surface of previously ground axes was necessary either to produce a smaller axe from a large damaged or broken one or as the result of much usage. When the edge had been refurbished a number of times the cutting angle became too steep to be efficient, so to produce, once more, the optimum cutting angle and preserve the symmetry of the axe, the overall thickness was reduced. This would lighten the axe and mean that it would take a little longer to fell a tree. Bruce Mitford (1938, 282) considered this practice to be connected with the waning of the polished axe trade in late Neolithic times, although this seems no good reason for deliberately reflaking the surface of an older but more efficient ground axe.

NOTES ON THE CATALOGUE

Parishes are in Gloucestershire unless otherwise stated, and are listed in alphabetical order in their counties. Parish boundaries as shown in the First Edition of the O.S. 1:25 000 maps issued between 1946 and about 1952, are those which have been used, while the country boundaries used were those in existence prior to April 1974.

Axes and their fragments are numbered consecutively in each parish except in the case of the Royce and Wilson collections which are placed at the end of their respective counties, while unprovenanced 'Cotswolds' are at the end. In almost every case the exact find spot of the flint is unknown and for that reason the National Grid Reference given is often the best that can be derived from the information on the specimen, box, or in fragmentary written records; usually a farm, hamlet, or centre of a village. Hence the prefix c. (circa). The principal exceptions to this are the Falconer and Witchell collections where the fields from which the flints were obtained are in many cases known.

Where a dimension has 'curved' applied to it, it signifies that the dimension is of the maximum thickness of flint on that specimen, not the maximum figure obtainable. When a dimension is locally exaggerated, because its maximum thickness is due to a bulb of percussion, it is indicated by 'b.o.p'. 'm.f.d.' indicates that the specimen was mounted for display in such a position that the taking of measurements was impossible.

In such cases where the only dimensions were recorded in the Imperial system the converted metric figures are shown in brackets. Weights are given to the nearest gram; again, those in brackets are converted figures. Only the complete or nearly complete axes were weighed.

'Type' refers to the finish of the axe, i.e. Flaked (F) or Ground (G) or Flaked and Ground (F+G). Those axes which have been flaked all over subsequent to grinding are listed as (G+F). However in the case of small fragments with areas of grinding it is assumed that they came from an axe which was ground all over.

Descriptions given in inverted commas are derived from written sources and are usually the only known references to the axe in question.

Identification marks include both numbers/letters which appear on the flints themselves, museum numbers and excavation catalogue numbers, while Ordnance Survey Antiquity numbers and written references are expanded in the bibliography. The series of bracketed numbers for LN 56 to 95 have been applied to aid identification for this survey. They are known to have been found for the most part, in the same fields as the rest of the Witchell collection but that is all.

Abbreviations used for the present location of axes and fragments is as follows:-

AM	Ashmolean Museum, OXFORD.
BM	British Museum, LONDON.
BCM	City Museum, BRISTOL.
CAGM	Art Gallery and Museum, CHELTENHAM, Glos.
CM	Corinium Museum, CIRENCESTER, Glos.
DM	Devizes Museum, DEVIZES, Wilts.
GCM	Museum and Art Gallery, GLOUCESTER.
KSM	Kingswood School Museum, BATH.
MAEC	University Museum of Archaeology and Ethnology, CAMBRIDGE.
OCC	Oxford City and County Museum, Woodstock, OXFORD.
WCM	County Museum, WARWICK.
KB	K. Bowley, Church Farm, Ashton Keynes, SWINDON, Wilts.
AJB	A. J. Broome, Glenhelen, Brize Norton Road, Minster Lovell, OXFORD.
JAE	J. A. Evetts, Wood House, Tackley, OXFORD.
EWG	Mrs. E. W. Gander, Highcroft, Syde, Elkstone, CHELTENHAM, Glos.
FCI	F. C. Innocent, Little Long Grounds, Donnington, LECHLADE, Glos.
RWK	R. W. Knight, Castle Farm, Marshfield, CHIPPENHAM, Wilts.
PD	P. Dixon, Dept. of Classical and Archaeological Studies, The University, NOTTINGHAM.
GHS	G. H. Swainston, Glebe House, Naunton, CHELTENHAM, Glos.
SW	S. Willes, Ladbarrow Farm, Aldsworth, CHELTENHAM, Glos.
AW	A. Witchell, Boldridge Farm, Long Newnton, TETBURY, Glos.

CATALOGUE

No.	National Grid Reference of find-spot	Present location	Max. dimensions (mm) Length	width	thickness	Wt. (g)	Type	Description	Identification marks	References
Almondsbury (Am)										
1.	c. ST592820	BCM	76.5	64.0	29.5	–	G	Edge, oval cross section, flattened sides, light honey coloured, mottled light patina.	F 3819	
Alveston (Al)										
1.	ST634883	?	?	?	?	?	G	"Polished flint axe."		O.S. Ant. No. ST68 NW11
Ashley (As)										
1.	c. ST923935	AW	35.4	19.4	39.7	–	G	Body fragment from near butt, creamy patina, some iron staining, striae.	2	
2.	c. ST923935	AW	29.8	39.6	15.3	–	G	Face fragment, side possibly flattened, light grey, fire damaged, striae.	2	
3.	c. ST923935	AW	21.0	24.5	4.9	–	G	Face fragment, heavy white patina, trace iron staining.	2	
4.	c. ST923935	AW	20.5	9.0	3.5	–	G	Pointed fragment, white patina, some staining.	2	

No.	National Grid Reference of findspot	Present location	Max. dimensions (mm) Length	width	thickness	Wt. (g)	Type	Description	Identification marks	References
Ashley (As)										
5.	c. ST918950	AW	29.4	27.0	6.2	–	G	Face fragment, creamy patina, little staining, striae.	136	
6.	c. ST918950	AW	29.9	39.4	21.3	–	G	Face/side fragment, face profile flat, light grey, fire damaged, striae.	98	
7.	c. ST918950	AW	30.0	30.3	13.7	–	G	Edge/corner fragment, mottled grey, slight iron staining, striae.	L III April 1968	
8.	c. ST914952	AW	44.6	38.7	24.6	–	G	Fragment, polished area, creamy patina, trace iron staining, striae.	LVIII	
9.	c. ST926931	AW	17.5	20.5	4.8	–	G	Face fragment, white patina, trace iron staining, striae.	AM	
10.	c. ST926931	AW	24.0	17.2	3.9	–	G	Face fragment, mottled, white patina, some staining.	AM	
11.	c. ST926931	AW	39.0	32.0	12.0	–	G	Side fragment, rounded, white patina, mottled, some iron staining, striae.	Ashley Marsh AM	
12.	c. ST929930	AW	49.0	44.8	12.5	–	G	Scraper from face fragment, small polished area, vugh, white patina, trace iron staining.	AM3	

13.	c. ST929930	AW	51.8	12.5	5.8 (curved)	–	G	Fragment, white patina, trace iron staining, striae.	AM3
14.	c. ST929933	AW	28.0	35.5	24.0	–	G	Edge fragment, light grey, fire damaged, striae.	AM4
15.	c. ST929933	AW	23.5	21.0	31.2	–	G	Face fragment, light grey, fire damaged, striae.	AM4
16.	c. ST929933	AW	15.0	10.2	2.5	–	G	Face fragment, white patina, slight staining, striae.	AM4
17.	c. ST929933	AW	24.2	27.0	6.7	–	G	Face fragment, white patina, slight staining, striae.	AM4
18.	c. ST926940	AW	31.8	33.9	12.7	–	G	Face fragment, white patina, pronounced curvature, slight staining, striae.	180
19.	ST927944	AW	56.3	43.7	8.9	–	G	Face fragment, grey/buff patina, some iron staining, striae, secondary retouch.	BT (Roman site on spur)
20.	c. ST926931	AW	26.7	13.3	4.6	–	G	Edge fragment, reworked as a scraper, grey, striae.	AM
21.	c. ST929930	AW	50.4	40.5	23.0	–	G	Body fragment from near butt, rounded sides, mottled, white patina, trace iron staining, fire damaged.	AM3
22.	c. ST923935	AW	57.8	43.4	28.5	–	G	Face fragment, white patina, iron staining, striae.	2 Long Thong

No.	National Grid Reference of findspot	Present location	Max. dimensions (mm) Length	width	thickness	Wt. (g)	Type	Description	Identification marks	References
Avening (Av)										
1.	c. ST869982	SM	42.5	41.0	28.5	–	G	Hammerstone from body fragment, heavy white patina, striae.	68.80	
2.	c. ST863990	SM	54.3	46.5	25.3	–	G.&F.	Fragment, grey, white patina, some staining, striae.	46.2/189	
3.	c. ST863990	SM	15.7 (curved)	40.5	9.4	–	G	Edge fragment, heavy white patina, striae.	46.2/190	
4.	ST898964	AW	32.5	38.5	21.4	–	G	Rough core from body fragment, heavy white patina, iron staining, striae.	ST898964	
5.	ST887968	AW	35.0	21.8	15.9	–	G	Body fragment from near edge, plug of siliceous material, spots of iron stain.	ST887968	
Badgeworth (Bd)										
1.	SO928161	PD	129.9	62.1	33.0	300	G	Oval cross section, flattened on sides, mottled, white patina, small vugh, fine striae at right angles to axis about c. of g.	CH 2431	

2.	SO928161	PD	82.0	60.0	29.0	(142)	G	Adze from large axe fragment, pointed oval cross section, heavy white patina, S-profile edge, striae.	CH 3661	

Barnwood (Br)

1.	SO865179	GCM	57.5	37.0	22.8	–	G	Hammerstone from body fragment, heavy patina, ochreous staining, striae.	A 3292	Clifford et al., 1954, 187.

Bibury (Bb)

1.	c. SP115065	BCM	29.1	9.5	5.5	–	G	Fabricator from corner fragment, heavy white patina, slight iron staining.	6589 Ducie Coll.

Bisley-with-Lypiatt (BL)

1.	c. SO905060	SM	29.5	17.0	8.7	–	G	Face/side fragment from near edge, heavy white patina, striae.	46.9/124
2.	c. SO916042	SM	65.3	39.8	22.8	–	G	Face fragment, mottled grey, white patina, trace staining, striae.	LH
3.	c. SO916044	SM	42.1	41.5	17.8	–	G	Body fragment, heavy white patina, some staining, striae.	46.9/23

No.	National Grid Reference of findspot	Present location	Max. dimensions (mm) Length	width	thickness	Wt. (g)	Type	Description	Identification marks	References
Bisley-with-Lypiatt (BL)										
4.	c. SO877056	CAGM	48.5	22.4	8.2 (curved)	–	G	Side/face fragment reworked as a scraper, heavy white patina, staining, striae.	20-4, C.A.W. (13) 1931.23	Paine Coll. 301
Brimpsfield (Bi)										
1.	c. SO928134	GCM	31.2	50.6	16.5	–	G	Edge/corner fragment, oval cross section, flattened side, white patina, some staining	A 3067 (A) Lewis Coll.	
2.	c. SO928134	GCM	32.3	61.5	18.6	–	G	Edge/corner fragment, oval cross section, flattened side, white patina.	A 3067 (B) Lewis Coll.	
3.	c. SO928134	GCM	38.4	45.9	20.5	–	G	Body fragment, oval cross section, grey, light patina, striae.	A 3067 (C) Lewis Coll.	
4.	c. SO928134	GCM	41.1	43.1	11.1	–	G	Face fragment, heavy white patina, some staining, striae.	A 3072 (7)	
5.	c. SO939127	CAGM	26.5	31.1	14.9	–	G	Butt, oval cross section, flattened sides, grey, light creamy patina, some iron staining, striae.	Brimpsfield	

Brockworth (Bo)

1. c. SO89 16	GCM	116.5	58.3	30.8	229	G	Oval cross section, damaged butt, mottled dark grey, mottled brown patina, striae, polished area near edge.	A 2989 304/1951

Cam (Cm)

1. SO744011	BCM	?	?	?	—	G	"A minute flake struck from an implement with a ground surface"	F4223-49 Smith, 1968, 24 O.S. Ant. No. SO70 SW4

Chalford (Cd)

1. SO899032	SM	179.0	65.5	35.7	547	G	Oval cross section, flattened sides, mottled grey, white patina, edge retouched by flaking, area of cortex, striae.	55.11 O.S. Ant. No. SO80 SE33
2. c. SO900038	?	?	?	?	?	?	"Of the flints there are... an axe".	Burton, 1929, 253

Chedworth (Ct)

1. SP031132	?	?	?	?	?	?	"Flint axe found 1916".	O.S. Ant. No. SP01 SW5
2. SP038132	?	?	?	?	?	G	"Polished flint axe found 1920".	O.S. Ant. No. SP01 SW6

No.	National Grid Reference of findspot	Present location	Max. dimensions (mm) Length	width	thickness	Wt. (g)	Type	Description	Identification marks	References
Cheltenham (Ch)										
1.	c. SO933234	CAGM	185.0	61.0	33.3	(517)	G	Oval cross section, squared sides, edge is light grey and polished, butt is dark grey and ground.	1947.98	
Cherington (Ce)										
1.	c. ST898984	SM	30.0	25.8	6.0 (curved)	–	G	Scraper from face fragment, light grey, white patina, striae.		
2.	c. ST916961	AW	24.8	19.3	3.4 (curved)	–	G	Face fragment, grey, striae.	TC 1	
3.	c. ST916961	AW	30.5	40.5	5.5	–	G	Face fragment, heavy white patina, speckled grey/brown, striae.	TC 1	
4.	c. ST916961	AW	21.3	19.7	5.0 (curved)	–	G	Side/face fragment, mottled grey, striae.	TC 1	
5.	c. ST916961	AW	31.7	28.1	6.7 (curved)	–	G	Face fragment, heavy white patina, some staining, polished.	TC 1	
6.	c. ST916961	AW	30.0	32.2	16.1 (curved)	–	G	Side/face fragment, heavy white patina, slight staining, striae.	TC 1	

7.	c. ST916961	AW	24.5	29.5	6.0 (curved)	–	G	Face fragment, heavy white patina, slight staining, polished, fine striae.	TC 1
8.	c. ST916961	AW	32.8	25.0	6.9 (b.o.p.)	–	G	Face fragment, heavy white patina, slight iron staining, striae, secondary retouch.	TC 1
9.	c. ST916961	AW	23.0	23.4	4.0	–	G	Face fragment, heavy white patina, speckled grey/brown.	TC 1
10.	c. ST916961	AW	14.9	26.8	3.5	–	G	Face fragment, heavy white patina, polished, fine striae.	TC 1
11.	c. ST916961	AW	21.5	16.5	4.0	–	G	Face/side fragment, heavy white patina, speckled grey/brown, striae.	TC 1
12.	c. ST916961	AW	39.7	41.5	23.5	–	G	Thin butt, oval cross section, rounded sides, mottled light grey, light patina, patches of cortex, striae.	TC 1
13.	c. ST916961	AW	53.5	62.5	31.0	–	G	Body fragment from near edge, oval cross section, rounded sides, heavy white patina, patches of cortex, fossil Micraster, striae.	TC 1
14.	c. ST916961	AW	(18.0)	?	(4.5)	–	G	Edge fragment.	TC 1
15.	c. ST916961	AW	26.3	21.9	11.4	–	G	Face fragment, grey, polished.	TC 1
16.	c. ST916961	AW	24.0	15.2	12.5 (curved)	–	G	Corner fragment, heavy white patina, polished.	Witchell, 1973

No.	National Grid Reference of findspot	Present location	Max. dimensions (mm) Length	width	thickness	Wt. (g)	Type	Description	Identification marks	References
Cherington (Ce)										
17.	c. ST916961	AW	37.8	37.3	5.5	–	G	Face fragment, heavy white patina, speckled grey/brown, striae.		
18.	c. ST916961	AW	32.7	20.1	6.4 (b.o.p.)	–	G	Corner fragment, heavy white patina, some staining, striae.		
19.	c. ST916961	AW	20.0	16.0	6.6	–	G	Face fragment, heavy white patina, some staining, striae.		
20.	c. ST916961	AW	18.0	22.7	3.5	–	G	Edge fragment, heavy white patina, speckled grey/brown, striae.		
21.	c. ST916961	AW	25.0	20.0	8.0	–	G	Face fragment, heavy white patina, some staining, striae.		
22.	c. ST916961	AW	32.5	18.7	6.2 (curved)	–	G	Face fragment, grey, white patina, secondary retouch.		
23.	c. ST916961	AW	25.2	27.0	7.0	–	G	Side/face fragment, heavy white patina, patch of cortex, some staining.		
24.	c. ST916961	AW	34.5	29.7	5.7	–	G	Face fragment, grey, white patina, striae, polished area.		
25.	c. ST916961	AW	20.5	35.7	8.5	–	G	Face fragment, heavy white patina, speckled grey/brown, striae.		

#	Location						Description
26.	c. ST916961	AW	24.0	16.8	2.7	–	G	Face fragment, heavy white patina, slight staining, striae.
27.	c. ST916961	AW	12.3	19.7	6.2	–	G	Face fragment, grey, white patina, striae.
28.	c. ST916961	AW	19.5	17.3	3.0 (curved)	–	G	Face fragment, grey, white patina, striae.
29.	c. ST916961	AW	11.4	11.4	2.3	–	G	Face fragment, heavy white patina, striae.
30.	c. ST916961	AW	14.8	15.2	3.3	–	G	Face fragment, heavy white patina, some staining, striae.
31.	c. ST916961	AW	7.0	16.0	1.2	–	G	Face fragment, heavy creamy patina, striae, polished.
32.	c. ST916961	AW	14.7	10.9	2.0 (b.o.p.)	–	G	Face fragment, grey, light patina, striae.
33.	c. ST916961	AW	13.4	13.4	2.3	–	G	Face fragment, heavy white patina, speckled grey/brown, striae, polished.
34.	c. ST916961	AW	15.0	13.7	1.4 (b.o.p.)	–	G	Face fragment, heavy white patina, staining, polished.
35.	c. ST916961	AW	15.7	10.9	2.0	–	G	Face fragment, heavy white patina, striae.
36.	c. ST916961	AW	34.4	29.5	6.8	–	G	Face fragment, light grey, light patina, striae, flaking scars visible.

No.	National Grid Reference of findspot	Present location	Max. dimensions (mm) Length	width	thickness	Wt. (g)	Type	Description	Identification marks	References
Cherington (Ce)										
37.	c. ST916961	AW	19.0	16.8	3.8 (curved)	–	G	Face fragment, grey, striae, fire damaged.		
38.	c. ST916961	AW	22.3	22.7	2.5 (curved)	–	G	Face fragment, grey, striae, polished.		
39.	c. ST916961	AW	27.6	44.5	8.6 (curved)	–	G	Body fragment, mottled grey, light patina, striae.		
40.	c. ST916961	AW	15.7	17.3	4.8	–	G	Face/side fragment, light patina, striae.		
41.	c. ST916961	AW	12.3	33.2	5.5	–	G	Face fragment, grey, light patina, striae.		
42.	c. ST914957	AW	29.5	27.9	19.5	–	G	Face fragment, heavy white patina, stained, striae, fire damaged.	TC 2	
43.	c. ST914957	AW	26.3	23.8	4.6 (curved)	–	G	Face fragment, heavy white patina, speckled grey/brown, buff stain.	TC 2	
44.	c. ST914957	AW	28.3	11.3	4.1	–	G	Side fragment, heavy white patina, little staining, flattened.	TC 2	
45.	c. ST914957	AW	16.0	32.2	11.3 (curved)	–	G	Face fragment, heavy white patina, speckled grey/brown, striae.	TC 2	

No.	Grid Ref							Description	Ref
46.	c. ST914957	AW	30.0	19.5	7.7 (curved)	–	G	Flattened side fragment, heavy white patina, some staining, striae.	TC 2
47.	c. ST914957	AW	25.2	28.1	6.0 (curved)	–	G	Face fragment, mottled grey, light patina, striae.	TC 2
48.	c. ST914957	AW	34.5	54.6	6.9	–	G	Face fragment, heavy white patina, striae, secondary retouch.	TC 2
49.	c. ST914957	AW	34.3	35.0	15.8	–	G	Body fragment, mottled grey, light patina, striae, fire damaged.	TC 2
50.	c. ST912960	AW	(30.0)	(50.0)	(16.0)	–	G	Edge fragment.	TC 5

Coaley (Cy)

| 1. | c. SO772017 | SM | 22.9 | 27.2 | 8.9 (curved) | – | G | Face/side fragment, dark grey and buff. | Witchell, 1973 46.17/1 |

Coberley (Cb)

| 1. | c. SO944168 | MAEC | 50.0 | 32.0 | 16.5 | – | F | Thin butt, pointed oval cross section, white patina, cortex. | 23.42D |

Condicote (Cc)

| 1. | c. SP140300 | GHS | 148.7 | 58.9 | 27.2 | (285) | F & G | Thin butt, pointed oval cross section, heavy white patina, striae near edge. | L 190 |
| 2. | c. SP140300 | GHS | 28.9 | 41.0 | 14.5 | – | G | Body fragment, oval cross section, flattened sides, heavy white patina, striae. | L 190 |

No.	National Grid Reference of findspot	Present location	Max. dimensions (mm) Length	width	thickness	Wt. (g)	Type	Description	Identification marks	References
Condicote (Cc)										
3.	c. SP140300	GHS	54.7	32.8	14.6	–	G	Scraper from face fragment, heavy white patina, staining, striae.		L 190
4.	c. SP140300	GHS	19.8	14.0	4.5	–	G	Leaf shaped arrowhead from face fragment, heavy white patina, striae.		L 190
5.	c. SP140300	GHS	23.0	32.3	4.2 (curved)	–	G	Edge fragment, heavy white patina, striae.		L 190
6.	c. SP140300	GHS	35.8	28.0	18.5	–	G	Face fragment, heavy white patina, iron staining, striae.		L 190
7.	c. SP140300	GHS	71.0	48.2	25.3	–	G	Body fragment, flattened sides, grey, heavy white patina, striae.		L 190
8.	c. SP140300	GHS	35.0	26.5	7.8	–	G	Corner fragment, heavy white patina, little staining, striae.		L 190
9.	c. SP140300	GHS	28.8	23.2	3.6	–	G	Face fragment, grey, heavy white patina.		L 190
10.	c. SP140300	GHS	42.0	23.0	5.4 (curved)	–	G	Face fragment, heavy white patina, some staining, striae.		L 190

11.	c. SP140300	GHS	25.4	19.5	4.5	–	G	Rough arrowhead from face fragment, heavy white patina, little staining, striae.	L 190
12.	c. SP140300	GHS	24.6	25.9	3.3	–	G	Face fragment, heavy white patina, little staining, striae, polished.	L 190
13.	c. SP140300	GHS	26.0	25.5	4.0	–	G	Face fragment, heavy white patina, striae.	L 190
14.	c. SP140300	GHS	41.7	28.8	10.2	–	G	Face fragment, white patina, staining.	L 190
15.	c. SP140300	GHS	48.0	24.0	7.0	–	G	Fragment, heavy white patina, staining, striae.	L 190
16.	c. SP152283	CAGM	27.0	27.0	4.5	–	G	Face fragment, heavy white patina, some staining, striae.	1081
17.	c. SP152283	CAGM	16.2	21.5	6.0	–	G	Face/edge fragment, heavy creamy patina, trace staining, striae, secondary retouch.	1600
18.	c. SP152283	CAGM	46.5	41.1	10.1	–	G	Face fragment, pronounced curvature, white patina, some staining, striae.	1568, 1931:23. Paine Coll. 301

Cowley (Cw)

1.	c. SO938154	CAGM	38.0	17.5 (curved)	10.3	–	G	Edge fragment, light grey, heavy white patina, striae.	6685

No.	National Grid Reference of findspot	Present location	Max. dimensions (mm) Length	width	thickness	Wt. (g)	Type	Descriptions	Identification marks	References
Cranham (Cr)										
1.	c. SO919121	SM	28.7	21.8	6.6	–	G	Rough leaf shaped arrow-head from thin butt fragment, oval cross section, flattened sides, grey, white patina.	46.47/1-41	
Dowdeswell (Dw)										
1.	c. SO990179	CAGM	61.0	49.5	12.8	–	G	Discoidal knife from edge fragment, flaked over surface, heavy white patina, little staining, striae.	1. J.H. Carde Coll.	
2.	c. SO990179	CAGM	39.5	50.0	22.7	–	G	Corner fragment, edge battered, grey, white patina, slight staining, one face polished.	2. J.H. Carde Coll.	
3.	c. SP02 19	CAGM	30.0	26.3	7.9	–	G	Face fragment, white patina, some staining, striae.	6691, 1931/23 Paine Coll. 01	
Doynton (Dy)										
1.	ST721714	KSM	44.8	40.0	20.5	–	G	Thin butt fragment, oval cross section, flattened sides, white patina, some staining, striae.	F 68 (FH, 12238)	

No.	Grid ref	Mus.	L	W	Th	Other #	Cond.	Description	Ref.
2.	ST721714	KSM	31.6	26.0	7.3 (curved)	–	G	Scraper from face fragment, greyish patina, striae.	F 73 (FH, 4543)
3.	ST721714	KSM	67.2	49.0	34.2	–	G	Body fragment, white patina, some staining, striae, small polished area.	F 575 (FH, 10234)
4.	ST721714	KSM	24.0	22.1	4.5	–	G	Face fragment, creamy patina, some staining, striae.	F 1310 (FH, 91032)

Falfield (Fa)

No.	Grid ref	Mus.	L	W	Th	Other #	Cond.	Description	Ref.
1.	c. ST68 93	BCM	?	?	?	?	G	"A polished flint axe found in a garden".	Grinsell, 1968, 64 O.S. Ant. No. ST69 SE7

Frocester (Fr)

No.	Grid ref	Mus.	L	W	Th	Other #	Cond.	Description	Ref.
1.	c. SO794027	GCM	66.0	41.2	24.4	–	G	Thin butt, oval cross section, flattened sides, heavy creamy patina, iron staining, striae.	32/1967
2.	Aggsbarrow Field	SM	36.7	16.7	m.f.d.	–	G	Side/face fragment, grey, white patina, some staining.	

Gloucester (Gl)

No.	Grid ref	Mus.	L	W	Th	Other #	Cond.	Description	Ref.
1.	c. SO82 18	MAEC	137.0	63.0	30.0	289	G	Thin butt, flattened oval cross section, flattened sides, grey, mottled brown patina, damaged edge.	22.105 Spencer Perceval Coll.

No.	National Grid Reference of findspot	Present location	Max. dimensions (mm) Length	width	thickness	Wt. (g)	Type	Description	Identification marks	References
Gloucester (Gl)										
2.	c. SO83 18	GCM	121.0	55.5	30.0	219	F & G	Oval cross section, rounded sides, mottled dark brown patina, damaged edge.	A 2995	
3.	c. SO83 20	GCM	185.0	65.0	38.3	(454)	F	Pointed oval cross section, mottled grey, patches of cortex, striae on one side.	A 3122 68/1954	A. Watts Coll.
4.	c. SO83 20	GCM	120.8	64.3	28.2	(227)	G	Thin butt, oval cross section, flattened sides, mottled grey, patches of cortex, striae.	A 3123 68/1954	A. Watts Coll.
Hatherop (Ha)										
1.	SP165088	SW	25.0	15.7	7.3	–	G	Side/face fragment, heavy white patina, some iron staining, striae.		
Henbury (He)										
1.	c. ST566781	MAEC	55.0	48.0	28.0	–	G	Body fragment, oval cross section, flattened sides, creamy white patina.	22.108 Spencer Perceval Coll.	
2.	c. ST54 78	MAEC	80.0	52.0	27.5	–	G	Body fragment, flattened sides, grey/white, fire damaged.	22.233 J	

Horsley (Ho)

1. c. ST833981	SM	71.7	33.6	18.9	–	G	Thin butt, oval cross section, flattened sides, mottled brown, creamy patina, striae.	Nupend Farm.
2. c. ST820981	SM	17.8	20.2	3.8	–	G	Edge fragment, heavy white patina, striae.	63.79

Kempsford (Ke)

1. c. SP150003	CAGM	89.0	66.0	30.0	–	G	Edge fragment, flattened oval cross section, rounded sides, brown, heavy white patina, stained, striae, groove along one face.	1972.150 Fowler & Miles, 1972, 13

Kingscote (Ki)

1. c. ST818963	SM	52.7	37.9	24.3	–	G	Face fragment, heavy white patina, striae.	46.34/26

Long Newnton (LN)

1. c. ST922933	AW	27.8	35.5	14.8	–	G	Face fragment, trace of a rounded side, pronounced curvature, grey, striae, fire damaged.	1 Gracie, 1942, 183
2. c. ST922933	AW	31.2	26.5	35.0	–	G	Side/face fragment, flattened side, white patina, some iron staining, striae, fire damaged.	1
3. c. ST922933	AW	30.0	19.2	6.2 (b.o.p.)	–	G	Side fragment, heavy white patina, striae.	1

No.	National Grid Reference of findspot	Present location	Max. dimensions (mm)			Wt. (g)	Type	Description	Identification marks	References
			Length	width	thickness					

Long Newnton (LN)

No.	National Grid Reference of findspot	Present location	Length	width	thickness	Wt. (g)	Type	Description	Identification marks	References
4.	c. ST922933	AW	19.5	55.7	16.0	–	G	Face fragment, grey, white patina, ground cortex, striae.	64	Footpath ground.
5.	c. ST921936	AW	35.5	27.0	9.5	–	G	Corner fragment, heavy white patina, some staining, striae.	3	
6.	c. ST921936	AW	15.5	24.8	4.9	–	G	Face fragment, heavy white patina, little staining, striae, polished.	3	
7.	c. ST921936	AW	28.2	37.8	16.3	–	G	Face fragment, grey, striae, fire damaged.	3	
8.	c. ST921936	AW	21.7	35.5	17.5	–	G	Side/Face fragment, flattened sides, heavy white patina, striae, fire damaged.	3	
9.	c. ST921936	AW	38.4	44.0	13.6	–	G	Side fragment, rounded sides, white patina, staining, striae.	236	
10.	c. ST916943	AW	39.9	35.2	22.1	–	G	Thin butt, oval cross section, grey, striae, fire damaged.	LI	
11.	c. ST916943	AW	24.8	13.0	3.8	–	G	Face fragment, creamy patina, some staining, striae, secondary retouch.	LI	

#									
12.	c. ST916943	AW	45.5	31.4	21.5	–	G	Body fragment, light grey, white patina, little iron staining, striae, vugh in one face, one end flaked to give a rough edge.	LI
13.	c. ST916943	AW	50.7	37.1	20.3	–	G	Face fragment, white patina, some iron staining, striae.	LI
14.	c. ST916943	AW	51.2	41.5	22.1	–	G	Thin butt, oval cross section, mottled grey, patina stained, striae, fire damaged, most of surface has flaked off.	LI
15.	c. ST916943	AW	34.7	27.8	19.3	–	G	Edge fragment, white patina, some iron staining, striae.	177
16.	c. ST916943	AW	14.1	18.7	3.5	–	G	Face fragment, white patina, some staining, striae.	186
17.	c. ST913944	AW	20.5	16.4	3.8 (curved)	–	G	Corner fragment, creamy patina, little staining, striae.	LII
18.	c. ST913944	AW	25.4	9.9	3.0	–	G	Side fragment, flattened side, creamy patina, little staining, striae.	LII
19.	c. ST913944	AW	21.8	19.6	3.6	–	G	Edge fragment, creamy patina, little staining, striae.	LII
20.	c. ST913944	AW	24.9	15.5	2.6	–	G	Face fragment, light grey patina, striae.	LII
21.	c. ST913944	AW	18.0	6.2	31.7	–	G	Edge fragment, mottled, white patina, trace iron staining.	LII

No.	National Grid Reference of findspot	Present location	Max. dimensions (mm) Length	width	thickness	Wt. (g)	Type	Description	Identification marks	References
Long Newnton (LN)										
22.	c. ST913944	AW	39.5	28.5	9.2	–	G	Side fragment, creamy patina, staining, striae.	LII	
23.	c. ST913944	AW	68.0	22.5	22.4	–	G	Body fragment, creamy patina, some iron staining, striae.	202	
24.	c. ST922941	AW	27.8	34.3	8.0	–	G	Face fragment, marked curvature, white patina, some staining, striae.	LIV	
25.	c. ST922941	AW	32.5	24.9	6.7	–	G	Face/side fragment near corner, white patina, some staining, striae, flattened sides, marked curvature, secondary retouch.	LIV	
26.	c. ST922941	AW	16.6	28.6	4.4	–	G	Face fragment, marked curvature, white patina, some staining, striae, secondary retouch.	LIV	
27.	c. ST922941	AW	19.8	16.9	2.4 (curved)	–	G	Edge fragment, stained patina, striae.	LIV	
28.	c. ST922941	AW	5.0	16.5	9.9	–	G	Side/face fragment, white patina, some staining, rounded sides, striae.	LIV	

29.	c. ST922941	AW	23.7	18.7	6.8 (curved)	–	G	Face fragment, white patina, some staining, striae.	LIV
30.	c. ST922941	AW	25.5	12.9	3.5	–	G	Face fragment, light brown/grey, white patina, some staining, striae, secondary retouch.	LIV
31.	c. ST922941	AW	21.4	25.6	5.2 (curved)	–	G	Face fragment, creamy patina, some iron staining, striae.	LIV
32.	c. ST916947	AW	37.5	26.0	9.9	–	G	Side/face fragment, white patina, some staining, striae.	LVI
33.	c. ST916947	AW	19.6	17.0	19.0	–	G	Face fragment, stained patina, striae, polished, fire damaged.	LVI
34.	c. ST916947	AW	25.8	17.7	16.7	–	G	Side/face fragment near corner, white patina, some staining, striae.	LVI
35.	c. ST916947	AW	28.0	29.9	7.0	–	G	Face fragment, white patina, some staining, striae.	LVI
36.	c. ST916947	AW	25.0	31.0	3.8	–	G	Face fragment, white patina, some iron staining, striae, much-worn secondary retouch along one edge.	LVI
37.	c. ST924931	AW	43.4	36.7	8.1	–	G	Face fragment, mottled grey, cream patina, some iron staining, striae, ovate shape.	B 2 Barnfield.

No.	National Grid Reference of findspot	Present location	Max. dimensions (mm) Length	width	thickness	Wt. (g)	Type	Description	Identification marks	References
Long Newnton (LN)										
38.	c. ST924931	AW	34.2	41.5	11.4	–	G	Corner/face fragment, creamy patina, little staining, striae, polished.	228	
39.	c. ST924924	AW	27.2	23.5	8.6	–	G	Face fragment, creamy patina, little staining, striae.	Bb	
40.	c. ST924924	AW	34.2	22.9	8.2	–	G	Face/side fragment, mottled grey, white patina, little staining, rounded side, striae, secondary retouch.	143	
41.	c. ST924924	AW	35.0	38.3	12.8	–	G	Face fragment reworked as a scraper, white patina, staining, striae.	134	
42.	c. ST922930	AW	24.2	23.7	6.4	–	G	Face fragment, creamy patina, little staining, striae.	B	
43.	c. ST922930	AW	59.6	40.9	15.5	–	G	Face fragment, white patina, some iron staining, striae.	B	
44.	c. ST922930	AW	19.0	21.6	3.7	–	G	Face fragment, mottled white patina, some iron staining, striae.	B	
45.	c. ST922933	AW	45.7	42.7	21.7	–	G	Butt, mottled patina, trace iron staining, flattened sides, fire damaged.	109	

46.	ST922936	AW	35.5	51.2	12.5 (curved)	–	G	Face fragment, white patina, some staining, striae, polished.	ST922936
47.	c. ST927936	AW	31.0	26.7	5.7 (curved)	–	G	Face fragment, suggestion of a rounded side, white patina, little staining, striae.	12
48.	c. ST927936	AW	13.0	13.7	3.0	–	G	Face fragment, creamy patina, little staining, striae.	91
49.	c. ST910943	AW	37.5	47.0	15.5	–	G	Edge fragment, mottled white patina, some iron staining, striae.	153
50.	c. ST922941	AW	35.5	36.9	13.5	–	F	Butt, white patina, some iron staining.	LIV
51.	c. ST 91 94	AW	8.4	17.0	2.5	–	G	Face fragment, light grey, creamy/white patina, little staining, striae. secondary retouch.	L
52.	c. ST 91 94	AW	12.7	11.8	2.8	–	G	Face fragment from near corner, creamy patina, little staining, striae.	L
53.	c. ST 91 94	AW	34.0	28.4	8.3	–	G	Face fragment, creamy patina, some iron staining, striae.	L
54.	c. ST914933	AW	31.0	31.7	8.7	–	G	Face fragment, grey/white, light patina, polished.	3 NG

No.	National Grid Reference of findspot	Present location	Max. dimensions (mm) Length	width	thickness	Wt. (g)	Type	Description	Identification marks	References
Long Newnton (LN)										
55.	c. ST903915	AW	79.9	25.9	18.2	–	G	Body fragment from near butt of chisel or narrow axe, mottled grey with mottled brown surface, patch of cortex, rounded sides, striae.	140	
56.	(ST922930)	AW	13.9	13.1	2.1	–	G	Part of a b+t arrowhead from face fragment, creamy patina, striae.	(280)	
57.	(ST922930)	AW	12.7	30.7	13.7	–	G	Face fragment, white patina, some staining, striae.	(281)	
58.	(ST922930)	AW	19.1	25.5	10.0	–	G	Edge fragment, creamy patina, staining, striae.	(282)	
59.	(ST922930)	AW	19.0	23.3	3.8	–	G	Edge fragment, white patina, little staining, striae.	(283)	
60.	(ST922930)	AW	22.0	28.0	6.0 (curved)	–	G	Face fragment, heavy white patina speckled grey and brown, striae.	(284)	
61.	(ST922930)	AW	16.0	25.8	4.6	–	G	Face fragment, heavy white patina speckled grey and brown, striae.	(285)	
62.	(ST922930)	AW	12.2	13.8	2.4 (b.o.p.)	–	G	Face fragment from butt, heavy white patina speckled grey and brown, striae.	(286)	

#	Grid							Description	
63.	(ST922930)	AW	30.2	21.3	13.2	–	G	Face fragment, buff patina, some iron staining.	(287)
64.	(ST922930)	AW	27.6	29.4	16.8	–	F & G	Face/side fragment, flattened side, white patina, some iron staining, striae.	(288)
65.	(ST922930)	AW	24.1	28.5	14.8	–	G	Face fragment, grey/buff, striae, fire damaged.	(289)
66.	(ST922930)	AW	43.1	24.4	5.6	–	G	Face fragment, white patina, little staining, striae, secondary retouch.	(290)
67.	(ST922930)	AW	17.0	16.8	3.5	–	G	Face fragment, off-white patina, striae.	(291)
68.	(ST922930)	AW	36.5	15.0	15.5	–	G	Side fragment, rounded, mottled grey, striae, fire damaged.	(292)
69.	(ST922930)	AW	33.0	20.3	6.5	–	G	Face/side fragment, white patina, little staining, striae, tarry encrustation.	(293)
70.	(ST922930)	AW	24.6	19.8	5.2	–	G	Face fragment, off-white patina, little staining, striae.	(294)
71.	(ST922930)	AW	38.5	24.0	8.1	–	G	Side fragment, mottled, light patina, little staining, secondary retouch.	(295)
72.	(ST922930)	AW	30.0	24.0	6.5	–	G	Face/side fragment, white patina, some staining, striae.	(296)

No.	National Grid Reference of findspot	Present location	Max. dimensions (mm) Length	width	thickness	Wt. (g)	Type	Description	Identification marks	References
Long Newnton (LN)										
73.	(ST922930)	AW	15.0	16.5	11.6	–	G	Fragment of flattened side, mottled, light patina, some staining, striae.		(297)
74.	(ST922930)	AW	22.8	11.9	2.8	–	G	Face fragment, creamy patina, little staining, striae.		(298)
75.	(ST922930)	AW	28.6	25.0	13.0	–	F & G	Face/side fragment, mottled, light patina, little staining, striae.		(299)
76	(ST922930)	AW	30.8	31.1	8.5 (curved)	–	G	Face fragment, white patina, some staining, striae, fire damaged.		(300)
77.	(ST922930)	AW	17.1	25.8	6.2	–	G	Face fragment, buff patina, stained, striae.		(301)
78.	(ST922930)	AW	20.7	25.1	8.6	–	G	Face fragment, reworked as a scraper, light patina, some staining, striae.		(302)
79.	(ST922930)	AW	16.7	9.3	11.0	–	G	Side/face fragment, side flattened, face polished, light patina, little staining.		(303)
80.	(ST922930)	AW	24.9	19.4	3.9 (curved)	–	G	Face fragment, mottled, light patina, little staining, striae.		(304)

81.	(ST922930)	AW	24.4	18.0	4.6	–	G	Face fragment, white patina, little staining, striae. (305)
82.	(ST922930)	AW	24.4	22.4	4.5	–	G	Face fragment, mottled, light patina, striae. (306)
83.	(ST922930)	AW	28.2	30.7	5.5	–	G	Face fragment, light patina, some staining, striae. (307)
84.	(ST922930)	AW	23.7	26.6 (curved)	6.5	–	G	Face/side fragment, light grey, white patina, little staining, flattened side. (308)
85.	(ST922930)	AW	3.2 (curved)	17.8	12.3	–	G	Face/side fragment, white patina, little staining, striae. (309)
86.	(ST922930)	AW	23.8	10.7	10.0	–	G	Rounded side fragment from near butt, white patina, striae. (310)
87.	(ST922930)	AW	20.5	18.0	6.6	–	G	Face fragment, off-white patina, little staining, striae. (311)
88.	(ST922930)	AW	17.8	18.0	4.1	–	G	Face fragment, off-white patina, little staining, striae. (312)
89.	(ST922930)	AW	30.4	41.0	24.2	–	G	Body fragment, reflaked so now appears to be edge end of small flaked axe, light grey, white patina, some staining. (313)
90.	(ST922930)	AW	12.3	17.3	2.3	–	G	Face fragment, cream patina, some staining, striae. (314)
91.	(ST922930)	AW	26.8	17.1	4.4	–	G	Face/side fragment from near butt, flattened sides, creamy patina, some staining, striae. (315)

No.	National Grid Reference of findspot	Present location	Max. dimensions (mm) Length	width	thickness	Wt. (g)	Type	Description	Identification marks	References
Long Newnton (LN)										
92.	(ST922930)	AW	20.0	16.6	3.7	–	G	Face fragment, grey/cream, light patina, light staining, striae, secondary retouch.	(316)	
93.	(ST922930)	AW	14.1	14.9	4.2	–	G	Side/face fragment, white patina, slight staining, striae.	(317)	
94.	(ST922930)	AW	23.7	13.5	5.5	–	G	Side/face fragment, white patina, slight staining, striae.	(318)	
95.	(ST922930)	AW	15.4	12.1	3.4	–	G	Face fragment, white patina, slight staining, curved striae.	(319)	
Lower Swell (LS)										
1.	c. SP174255	BM	62.5	40.0	16.0	39	F	'Pear drop' shaped, pointed oval cross section, small flat on edge, cream/honey patina.	439 Sturge Coll.	Gettins et al., 1953, 38
Marshfield (Ma)										
1.	c. ST795745	BCM	34.3	27.7	6.0	–	G	Face fragment, white patina, striae.	F 3562	
2.	c. ST768718	?	?	?	?	–	G	"...butt end of polished axe...."		O.S. Ant. No. ST77 SE6 Knight, 1973.

3.	c. ST771742	RWK	27.3	23.2	5.8 (curved)	–	G	Face fragment, white patina, some staining, striae.	Home Close
4.	c. ST771742	RWK	13.8 (curved)	37.0	5.3	–	G	Face fragment, heavy white patina, some staining, striae.	Home Close
5.	c. ST771742	RWK	42.2	41.8	22.0	–	G	Face/side fragment, mottled grey patina, some iron staining, striae, fire damaged.	Home Close

Minchinhampton (Mn)

1.	c. ST884998	GCM	63.3	58.9	30.7	–	G	Edge fragment, oval cross section, grey, heavy white patina, patch of cortex on side, striae.	A 3053 Playne Coll.
2.	c. SO872007	SM	28.4	43.0	16.5	–	G	Body fragment near butt, oval cross section, flattened sides, heavy white patina, some staining.	M

Miserden (Ms)

1.	c. SO919103	GCM	43.7	34.0	28.5	–	G	Small core from body fragment, heavy white patina, slight staining, striae.	A 3385
2.	c. SO919103	GCM	39.9	28.7	23.1	–	G	Small core from body fragment, heavy white patina, slight staining, striae.	A 3385a
3.	c. SO919103	GCM	29.6	24.5	11.8	–	G	Body fragment near butt, sides much abraded, grey, striae, fire damaged.	A 3386

No.	National Grid Reference of findspot	Present location	Max. dimensions (mm) Length	width	thickness	Wt. (g)	Type	Description	Identification marks	References
Miserden (Ms)										
4.	c. SO939079	SM	30.5	36.9	13.4	–	G	Thin butt, small area of cortex, heavy white patina, some iron staining, striae.	56.139	
5.	c. SO939079	SM	39.3	10.5	7.1	–	G	Corner fragment, flattened side, mottled grey, light patina, striae.	56.139	
6.	c. SO914093	CAGM	12.5	11.4	12.4	–	G	Fragment, white patina, polished.	102	
7.	c. SO914093	CAGM	35.2	25.7	9.0	–	G	Face fragment, creamy patina, some staining, striae, secondary retouch.	728	
8.	c. SO914093	CAGM	36.3	35.2	21.3	–	G	Face fragment, heavy white patina, some staining, striae.	314	
9.	c. SO914093	SM	54.9	43.8	22.5	–	G	Fragment, patches of cortex, heavy white patina, some staining, striae.	Camp	
North Nibley (NN)										
1.	ST74 95	GCM	145.9	64.0	33.9	359	G	Thin butt, oval cross section, rounded sides, white patina, slight staining, polished near edge.	A 2991	Lucy, 1892, 29 Crawford, 1925, 9 O.S. Ant. No. ST79 NW4

2.	c. ST765965	SM	43.7	45.5	18.5	–	G	Body fragment, oval cross section, flattened sides, heavy white patina, some staining, striae.	46.23/13

Prestbury (Pr)

1.	c. SP003234	CAGM	22.5	38.2	15.5	–	G	Thin butt, oval cross section, heavy white patina, some staining, striae.	1
2.	c. SP003234	CAGM	25.6	15.7	3.5 (curved)	–	G	Scraper from face fragment, mottled, creamy patina, striae.	2
3.	c. SP003234	CAGM	55.5	39.2	20.4	–	G	Tapered butt, rough flaked edge, heavy white patina, some iron staining.	3
4.	c. SP003234	CAGM	82.5	45.4	13.0 (curved)	–	F	Thin butt, mottled grey, light patina, some iron staining.	4
5.	c. SP003234	CAGM	57.0	57.8	26.5	–	G	Scraper from body fragment, creamy patina, iron stained, striae.	5
6.	c. SP003234	CAGM	26.8	28.5	4.3	–	G	Rough barbed and tanged arrowhead from face fragment, heavy patina, slight staining, striae.	6
7.	c. SP003234	CAGM	49.5	40.0	30.0	–	G	Tapered butt, thick oval section, grey, off-white patina, some iron staining, striae.	7

No.	National Grid Reference of findspot	Present location	Max. dimensions (mm) Length	width	thickness	Wt. (g)	Type	Description	Identification marks	References
Prestbury (Pr)										
8.	c. SP003234	CAGM	49.2	41.9	15.1	–	F	Tapered butt, grey, heavy white patina.		8
9.	c. SP003234	CAGM	38.4	30.3	17.1	–	F	Tapered butt, grey, heavy white patina, some staining.		9
10.	c. SP003234	CAGM	44.3	36.4	21.2	–	G	Corner fragment, flattened sides, grey, heavy white patina, striae, polished near edge.		10
11.	c. SP003234	CAGM	20.9	28.4	11.3	–	G	Corner fragment, edge blunted.		11
12.	c. SP003234	CAGM	64.5	11.3 (curved)	20.6	–	G	Corner fragment, rounded side, heavy white patina, staining, striae.		12
13.	c. SP003234	CAGM	45.2	6.3 (curved)	11.4	–	G	Corner fragment, flattened side, heavy white patina, some staining, striae.		13
14.	c. SP003234	CAGM	42.6	14.8	19.9	–	G	Scraper from side fragment, pointed oval cross section, heavy white patina, some staining, striae.		14
15.	c. SP003234	CAGM	13.0	32.8	8.2	–	G	Edge fragment, buff patina, striae, polished.		15

16.	c. SP003234	CAGM	18.0	45.5	11.0	–	G	Chipped edge fragment, dark grey, striae, fire damaged.	16
17.	c. SP003234	CAGM	25.4	39.1	19.0	–	G	Face/side fragment, flattened side, dark grey, striae, fire damaged.	17
18.	c. SP003234	CAGM	32.2	28.5	12.3	–	G	Face/side fragment, flattened side, dark grey, striae, fire damaged.	18
19.	c. SP003234	CAGM	45.0	47.3	22.7	–	G	Face/side fragment, flattened side, dark grey, light patina, some staining, striae, fire damaged, battered ends.	19
20.	c. SP003234	CAGM	63.5	74.3	29.0	–	G	Large scraper from body fragment (restored), battered, off-white patina, some staining, striae, polished.	20
21.	c. SP003234	CAGM	28.2	49.6	18.3	–	G	Face/side fragment from near edge, roughly flaked edge, plug of siliceous material, white patina, some staining, striae.	21
22.	c. SP003234	CAGM	43.8	37.4	26.0	–	G	Corner fragment, asymmetric curvature of faces, edge re-flaked prior to breaking, white patina, some staining, striae.	22

No.	National Grid Reference of findspot	Present location	Max. dimensions (mm) Length	width	thickness	Wt. (g)	Type	Description	Identification marks	References
Prestbury (Pr)										
23.	c. SP003234	CAGM	42.3	54.1	13.0 (curved)	–	G	Scraper from face fragment, heavy white patina, some iron staining.	23	
24.	c. SP003234	CAGM	33.1	34.5	21.4	–	G	Body fragment near butt, rounded sides, heavy white patina, striae.	24	
25.	c. SP003234	CAGM	49.2	42.9	22.8	–	G	Face/side fragment, rounded sides, roughly flaked ends, heavy creamy patina, staining.	25	
26.	c. SP003234	CAGM	20.4	32.1	6.8	–	G	Face fragment, white patina, some staining, striae.	26	
27.	c. SP003234	CAGM	18.9	30.3	7.5	–	G	Face fragment, off-white patina, slight staining, striae.	27	
28.	c. SP003234	CAGM	49.4	25.9	9.1	–	G	Rough point from face/side fragment, flattened side, heavy white patina.	28	
29.	c. SP003234	CAGM	28.1	26.2	7.2	–	G	Face fragment, heavy creamy patina, striae.	29	
30.	c. SP003234	CAGM	30.4	30.8	7.0	–	G	Face fragment, off-white patina, trace staining, striae.	30	

No.							Description	
31.	c. SP003234	CAGM	27.0	32.0	6.2 (curved)	–	G	Face fragment, end battered, white patina, slight staining, striae.	31
32.	c. SP003234	CAGM	28.4	31.9	8.6	–	G	Face fragment, heavy creamy patina, some staining, striae.	32
33.	c. SP003234	CAGM	36.0	42.8	13.9 (b.o.p.)	–	G	Rough borer from face fragment, light grey patina, staining, striae, crazed surface.	33
34.	c. SP003234	CAGM	23.6	23.9	5.7 (curved)	–	G	Face fragment, pronounced curvature, mottled patina, staining, striae.	34
35.	c. SP003234	CAGM	30.5	25.1	7.1	–	G	Face/side fragment, flattened side, heavy white patina, slight staining, striae.	35
36.	c. SP003234	CAGM	25.3	23.1	6.2	–	G	Face/side fragment, flattened side, mottled, white patina, trace staining, striae.	36
37.	c. SP003234	CAGM	44.7	20.7	6.6	–	G	Rounded side fragment, mottled, white patina, trace staining. striae.	37
38.	c. SP003234	CAGM	38.0	23.5	7.9	–	G	side/face fragment, flattened side, heavy creamy patina, slight staining, striae.	38
39.	c. SP003234	CAGM	45.2	21.8	21.5	–	G	Side/face fragment, rounded side, light grey, heavy white patina, trace staining, striae.	39

No.	National Grid Reference of findspot	Present location	Max. dimensions (mm) Length	width	thickness	Wt. (g)	Type	Description	Identification marks	References
Prestbury (Pr)										
40.	c. SP003234	CAGM	43.5	45.4	18.7	–	G	Corner fragment, rounded side, mottled, white patina, striae.	3 J.H. Cardew Coll.	
Sevenhampton (Se)										
1.	c. SP002222	CAGM	29.0	27.4	7.0	–	G	Face/side fragment, rounded side, heavy white patina, some staining, secondary retouch.	6411	
South Cerney (SC)										
1.	c. SU041990	CM	127.0	65.0	30.5	(312)	F & G	Oval cross section, thin butt, flattened sides, edge reground, some flake scars visible, brown, white patina.	D100/6154	
Stinchcombe (Si)										
1.	c. ST74 98	GCM	85.5	56.9	30.0	136	G	Adze from large axe fragment, oval cross section, flattened sides, white patina.	A 2992	Anon., 1881, 214 Lucy, 1892, 29 Crawford, 1925, 9 O.S. Ant. No. ST79 NW7
2.	c. ST73 97	GCM	18.2	17.4	5.7 (curved)	–	G	Face fragment, heavy white patina, some staining, striae.	A5433	

Stonehouse (So)

#	Grid ref	Museum						Description	
1.	SO804054	SM	51.0	49.5	27.9	–	G	Thin butt, oval cross section, flattened sides, heavy white patina, some iron staining, striae.	3734
2.	c. SO805046	GCM	114.7	62.8	35.0	284	G	Oval cross section, flattened sides, butt/side damaged, mottled brown, striae.	A 2990

Stroud (Sr)

#	Grid ref	Museum						Description	
1.	c. SO85 05	CAGM	53.0	34.4	11.0	–	G	Scraper from face fragment, white patina, staining, striae.	21-22(12) 1931:23 E. Witchell/ Paine Coll. 301
2.	c. SO85 05	SM	48.6	41.0	27.7	–	G	Hammer stone from face/side fragment near butt, mottled grey, white patina, striae.	46.54/93
3.	c. SO85 05	SM	44.1	42.4	34.3	–	G	Side/face fragment, rounded side, heavy white patina, striae, fire damaged.	46.54/94
4.	c. SO85 05	SM	29.7	32.9	15.5	–	G	Corner fragment, heavy white patina, striae.	46.54/91
5.	c. SO85 05	SM	38.6	21.0	20.0	–	G	Fabricator from corner fragment, light grey, heavy white patina, striae.	46.54/92
6.	c. SO829057	SM	60.4	47.3	30.5 (curved)	–	G	Oval scraper from side/face fragment, mottled brown, striae.	62.173

No.	National Grid Reference of findspot	Present location	Max. dimensions (mm) Length	width	thickness	Wt. (g)	Type	Description	Identification marks	References
Syde (Sy)										
1.	SO959111	EWG	29.6	36.2	10.4	—	G	Face fragment, heavy white patina, some staining, striae.	X	
2.	SO955117	EWG	31.8	22.7	7.0 (curved)	—	G	Side/face fragment, heavy white patina, some staining, striae, secondary retouch.	P 760	
3.	SO949118	EWG	24.5	18.9	3.0	—	G	Face fragment, heavy white patina, polished.		
Temple Guiting (TG)										
1.	SP106297	CAGM	53.0	69.2	18.7	—	G	Flattened oval cross section, creamy white patina, striae, polished.		Brown, 1973
Thornbury (Th)										
1.	c. ST63 90	?	?	?	?	?	G	"A Neolithic flint instrument".		Griffiths, 1949/52, 305 O. S. Ant. No. ST69 SW9
Uley (Ul)										
1.	c. SO789000	?	(101.6)	(50.8)	?	?	?	"One of these axe heads... is of flint....".		Thurnham, 1854, 322
2.	SO789000	CAGM	(123.8)	.f.d.	m.f.d.	m.f.d.	G	White patina, striae, damaged.	1926:10	

57

Uley (U1)

3.	c. ST785990	CAGM	48.2	43.4	26.8	–	G	Crude scraper from body fragment, transverse break used as striking platform, patch of cortex, heavy white patina, staining, striae, polished.	22
4.	c. ST785990	CAGM	37.0	25.8	5.0	–	G	Scraper from face fragment, heavy white patina, staining striae.	14-3 1931:23 Paine Coll.
5.	c. ST785990	CAGM	29.3	36.7	9.0	–	G	Face fragment, pronounced curvature, heavy white patina, some staining, striae.	18-22 1931:23 Paine Coll. 301
6.	c. ST785990	CAGM	36.5	22.0	4.4 (curved)	–	G	Face fragment, mottled, white patina, some iron staining, striae, secondary retouch.	36
7.	c. ST785990	CAGM	50.2	37.4	15.8	–	G	Face fragment, light grey, heavy white patina, some iron staining.	38-8
8.	c. ST785990	CAGM	30.0	37.7	6.2 (curved)	–	G	Face fragment, heavy white patina, some staining, striae, polished.	38-22
9.	c. ST785990	CAGM	28.2	38.5	7.0	–	G	Face fragment, light grey, heavy white patina, some staining, striae.	39-12 1931:23 Paine Coll. 301
10.	c. ST785990	CAGM	40.4	41.0	13.9	–	G	Face/side fragment, heavy white patina, some staining, striae.	39-13

No.	National Grid Reference of findspot	Present location	Max. dimensions (mm) Length	width	thickness	Wt. (g)	Type	Description	Identification marks	References

Uley (U1)

No.	National Grid Reference of findspot	Present location	Length	width	thickness	Wt. (g)	Type	Description	Identification marks	References
11.	c. ST785990	CAGM	41.5	49.5	28.7	–	G	Face/side fragment, mottled grey, some iron staining, striae, rounded side, fire damaged.	47-1	
12.	c. ST785990	CAGM	37.0	31.8	7.5	–	G	Face fragment, heavy white patina, some staining, striae, polished area.	47-21 1931:23 Paine Coll. 301	
13.	c. ST785990	CAGM	29.2	33.2	10.8	–	G	Face/edge fragment, heavy white patina, some staining, striae.	47-27B	
14.	c. ST785990	CAGM	19.8	36.7	16.5	–	G	Side/face fragment, grey/white banded, light patina, striae, some iron staining.	49-11 1931:23 Paine Coll.	
15.	c. ST 785990	SM	23.0	21.5	3.5	–	G	Face fragment, white patina, striae.	3688	
16.	c. ST785990	SM	10.8	11.7	3.7	–	G	Corner fragment, mottled grey, white patina, striae.	63.78/24	
17.	c. SO789000	SM	29.4	26.5	7.5	–	G	Scraper from face fragment, grey, white patina, area of cortex.	46.57/1	
18.	c. ST789996	GCM	45.8	20.5	9.9	–	G	Face fragment, heavy white patina, some iron staining, striae.	3/1968	

Winstone (Wn)

1.	SO975097	EWG	27.0	21.5	5.0 (curved)	—	G	Face fragment, grey, white patina, some staining.	Bi 215
2.	SO950099	EWG	14.7	11.4	2.5	—	G	Face/side fragment, white patina, staining.	M 34

Withington (Wt)

1.	c. SO998159	CAGM	45.5	33.5	16.0	—	G	Thin butt, pointed oval cross section, heavy white patina, some staining	5 J. H. Cardew Coll.

Wotton-under-Edge (WUE)

1.	c. ST796967	GCM	14.0	41.0	24.0	—	G	Face fragment, pronounced curvature, heavy white patina, slight staining, striae.	92/1969

Royce Collection

1.	c. SP17 26	BCM	142.4	62.4	32.0	300	F	Rough out, pointed D-shaped cross section, one face flat, mottled grey, small areas of cortex.	562 M	Lucy, 1892, 30 Grinsell, 1964, 56
2.	c. SP17 26	BCM	64.0	16.0	8.0	—	G	Flattened side fragment, white patina, slight iron staining, striae.	562 M
3.	c. SP17 26	BCM	49.1	31.8	13.3	—	G	Body fragment from near butt, pointed oval cross section, grey, white patina, iron stain.	562 M

No.	National Grid Reference of findspot	Present location	Max. dimensions (mm) Length	width	thickness	Wt. (g)	Type	Description	Identification marks	References
Royce Collection										
4.	c. SP17 26	BCM	27.3	21.5	4.1 (curved)	–	G	Face fragment, heavy white patina, striae.	562 M	
5.	c. SP17 26	BCM	28.3	15.8	4.3	–	G	Face fragment, heavy white patina.	562 M	
6.	c. SP17 26	BCM	55.3	47.0	30.4	–	G	Thin butt, oval cross section, flattened sides, heavy patina, striae.	562 M	
7.	c. SP17 26	BCM	37.9	19.5	3.9 (curved)	–	G	L/s arrowhead from fragment, grey, white patina, striae, secondary retouch.	562 M	
8.	c. SP17 26	BCM	22.2	27.5	6.8	–	F	Thin butt, oval cross section, mottled light grey.	562 M	
9.	c. SP17 26	BCM	39.0	29.9	10.6 (curved)	–	F	Thin butt, oval cross section, light grey, white patina, slight staining.	562 M	
10.	c. SP17 26	BCM	53.3	28.3	17.6	–	F	Thin butt, oval cross section, heavy white patina, slight iron staining.	562 M	
11.	c. SP17 26	BCM	42.2	28.2	9.2	–	G	Face fragment, flattened ripples on polished area, black, heavy white patina, secondary retouch on long sides.	562 M	

12.	c. SP17 26	BCM	22.5	17.7	3.2 (curved)	–	G	Face fragment, heavy white patina, polished area.	562 M
13.	c. SP17 26	BCM	31.6	39.8	11.6	–	G	Face fragment, heavy white patina, slight iron staining, polished area, secondary retouch.	562 M
14.	c. SP17 26	AM	73.0	19.0	12.0	–	G	'Fabricator' from side fragment, flattened sides, heavy white patina.	Wilcox; 1963:1845
15.	c. SP17 26	AM	39.5	19.0	5.5	–	G	Double edged scraper from side fragment, steep retouch, striae, white patina.	1963:1861a

Asthal, Oxon. (At)

1.	c. SP30 12	AM	94.0	50.0	27.0	–	G	Body fragment, pointed oval cross section, grey, heavy white patina, striae, polished area.	1968:1792 Peake Coll.
2.	SP295108	AJB	33.7	18.7	4.6	–	G	Face fragment, white patina, some staining, striae.	II
3.	SP295108	AJB	17.2	26.9	5.6	–	G	Face fragment, white patina, some staining, striae, secondary retouch.	II
4.	c. SP290109	AJB	23.4	32.4	8.0	–	G	Face fragment, white patina, iron staining, striae.	F 6
5.	c. SP290109	AJB	19.6	22.8	4.0	–	G	Face fragment, white patina, some staining, striae.	F 6

No.	National Grid Reference of findspot	Present location	Max. dimensions (mm) Length	width	thickness	Wt. (g)	Type	Description	Identification marks	References
Asthal, Oxon. (At)										
6.	c. SP290109	AJB	19.5	12.0	2.7 (curved)	–	G	Face fragment, white patina, some staining, striae.	F 6	
7.	c. SP290109	AJB	47.3	18.5	7.5 (curved)	–	G	Face fragment, white/buff patina, stained, striae.	F 6	
Ascott-under-Wychwood, Oxon. (AUW)										
1.	SP300176	OCC	18.3	32.9	3.0	–	G	Face fragment, grey, white patina, striae.	917 (Chamber 3)	Selkirk, 1971, 10
2.	SP300176	OCC	24.4	17.4	4.0	–	G	Face fragment, grey, white patina, striae.	1380 (L 24)	
3.	SP300176	OCC	20.5	30.3	7.9	–	G	Face fragment, heavy white patina, striae.	1680 (Q 35)	
4.	SP300176	OCC	17.5	22.0	3.7	–	G	Edge fragment, grey, white patina, striae.	1705 (H 23)	
5.	SP300176	OCC	28.8	18.5	2.5 (curved)	–	G	Face fragment, mottled grey, white patina, striae.	1715 (G 25)	
6.	SP300176	OCC	18.2	9.4	1.1 (curved)	–	G	Face fragment, grey, white patina, striae.	1788 (O 25)	
7.	SP300176	OCC	24.7	13.8	2.7 (curved)	–	G	Face/side fragment, grey, white patina, striae.	1826 (N 26)	
8.	SP300176	OCC	16.7	19.6	2.8	–	G	Face fragment, grey, white patina, striae.	1853 (M 24)	

9.	SP300176	OCC	22.0	15.2	3.0 (curved)	—	G	Face fragment, grey, white patina, striae.	1859 (F 22)
10.	SP300176	OCC	15.8	15.7	1.5 (curved)	—	G	Face fragment, white patina, striae.	1875 (J 24)
11.	SP300176	OCC	22.2	33.4	3.9 (curved)	—	G	Fragment, white patina, striae.	1880 (F 24)
12.	SP300176	OCC	?	?	?	—	G	Fragment not available for inspection.	907 (P 23)

Aston Bampton, Oxon. (AB)

1.	c. SP358017	AM	122.0	38.0	23.3	142	G & F	Waisted profile, thin butt, pointed oval cross section, dark brown.	Loan 103

Begbroke, Oxon. (Be)

1.	c. SP479135	?	?	?	?	—	G	"....butt of a polished axe-head....".	Sturdy & Sutermeister, 1964/5, 190

Bloxham, Oxon. (Bl)

1.	c. SP436357	?	?	?	?	?	G	"Neolithic polished axe, described as chert....".	O.C.C. County Field Survey No. 5335

Bruern, Oxon. (Bu)

1.	SP259199	?	?	?	?	?	F & G	"...partially polished flint chisel....".	Brown, 1968, 138

No.	National Grid Reference of findspot	Present location	Max. dimensions (mm) Length	width	thickness	Wt. (g)	Type	Description	Identification marks	References
Cassington, Oxon. (Cs)										
1.	SP449101	AM	(5.0)	(22.0)	?	–	G	Edge fragment, white patina, fire damaged.	1944:141	Atkinson, 1947, 18
2.	c. SP449101	AM	128.3	27.3	19.1	90	G	Chisel, thin butt, pointed oval cross section, mottled light grey, white patina, striae.	1945:84	
Clanfield, Oxon. (Cf)										
1.	SP270015	AM	205.0	70.0	39.0	590	F	Rounded edge, thin butt, pointed oval cross section, grey, orange patina.	1956:973	Case, 1957, 104
Grafton & Radcot, Oxon. (GR)										
1.	c. SU285994	?	?	?	?	?	?	"Neolithic flint axehead found in the Thames....".		O.S. Ant. No. SU29 NE22 Manning & Leeds, 1920/1, 263
Great Tew, Oxon. (GT)										
1.	c. SP39 29	?	?	?	?	?	?	"Neolithic flint celt near French's Hollow."		Manning & Leeds, 1920/1, 244
Kiddington-with-Asterleigh, Oxon. (KA)										
1.	c. SP40 20	AM	62.5	38.0	26.0	–	G	Hammerstone from body fragment, oval cross section, broad flattened sides.	1968:939 Dillon Coll.	Dillon, 1875, 33

2.	c. SP40 20	AM	50.0	39.0	23.0	–	G	Thin butt, oval cross section, flattened sides, white patina.	1968:938 Dillon Coll.

Kencot, Oxon. (Kn)

1.	SP252072	FCI	(114.3)	(63.5)	(57.2)	(177)	G	Thin butt, oval section, flattened sides, flaking not ground out at butt, white patina.	Leeds, 1938, 168

Minster Lovell, Oxon. (ML)

1.	c. SP317124	AJB	47.8	38.2	24.7	–	G	Half of thin butt, white patina, striae, polished area, fire damaged.	PF
2.	c. SP317124	AJB	23.2	21.3	2.7 (curved)	–	G	Face fragment, white patina, some staining, striae.	PF
3.	c. SP317124	AJB	10.8	16.3	2.3	–	G	Face fragment, white patina, striae.	PF
4.	c. SP317124	AJB	29.2	41.2	19.6	–	G	Body fragment, depression in one face highly polished, white patina, staining.	PF
5.	c. SP332119	AJB	26.0	31.2	15.2	–	G	Side/face fragment, white patina, some staining, striae.	II
6.	c. SP330117	AJB	23.7	21.3	9.8	–	G	Thin butt of chisel, pointed oval cross section, grey, white patina, striae.	

No.	National Grid Reference of findspot	Present location	Max. dimensions (mm) Length	width	thickness	Wt. (g)	Type	Description	Identification marks	References
Sarsden, Oxon. (Sa)										
1.	c. SP291233	BM	41.5 tang 14.0	17.0 tang 9.0	7.0	–	G	Tanged arrowhead from side/face fragment, white patina, striae.	1905:89 Christy Coll.	
2.	c. SP291233	BCM	31.6	22.5	6.0	–	G	Scraper from side/face fragment, heavy white patina, some iron staining, striae.	6589 Ducie Coll.	
3.	c. SP291233	BCM	19.0	21.6	8.0	–	G	Thin butt, pointed oval cross section, light grey heavy white patina.	6589 Ducie Coll.	
4.	c. SP291233	BCM	41.2	23.1	6.4	–	G	Scraper from face fragment, heavy white patina, some iron staining	6589 Ducie Coll.	
5.	c. SP291233	BCM	25.5	27.5	9.8	–	G	Round scraper from face fragment, white patina, trace iron staining, polished area.	6589 Ducie Coll.	
6.	c. SP291233	BCM	36.7	31.2	11.3	–	F	Thin butt, pointed oval cross section, heavy white & grey patina, trace iron staining.	6589 Ducie Coll.	

Standlake, Oxon. (St)

No.	Grid Ref	Mus.	L	W	Th	Wt	Cond	Description	Acc.	Reference
1.	SP392045	AM	188.0	72.0	41.0	670	G	Thin rounded butt, oval cross section, flattened sides, rounded edge, light brown.	1962:100	Case & Sturdy, 1961/2, 338

Stanton Harcourt, Oxon. (SH)

No.	Grid Ref	Mus.	L	W	Th	Wt	Cond	Description	Acc.	Reference
1.	c. SP401055	AM	137.0	50.0	35.0	300	G	Thin butt, oval cross section, rounded sides, damaged edge, grey, white patina.	1948:93	Atkinson, 1948, 67
2.	SP406049	AM	?	?	?	–	G	"...irregular side scraper from polished implement... curvature suggests an axe."	1964:442/3	Hamlin, 1963, 2; Case, 1963, 19

Stonesfield, Oxon. (Sn)

No.	Grid Ref	Mus.	L	W	Th	Wt	Cond	Description	Acc.	Reference
1.	c. SP396183	AM	59.0	30.0	17.0	–	F	Thin butt, pointed oval cross section	1968:951 Dillon Coll.	Dillon, 1875, 33
2.	c. SP40 19	AM	50.5	45.0	19.5	–	G	Thin butt, oval cross section, white patina.	1968:953 Dillon Coll.	
3.	c. SP40 19	AM	73.0	30.0	16.0	–	G	Side fragment, white patina	1968:954 Dillon Coll.	

Tackley, Oxon. (Ta)

No.	Grid Ref	Mus.	L	W	Th	Wt	Cond	Description	Acc.	Reference
1.	c. SP47 21	JAE	38.2	42.2	16.8	–	G	Corner fragment of adze, oval cross section, heavy white patina, some iron staining.		

No.	National Grid Reference of findspot	Present location	Max. dimensions (mm) Length	width	thickness	Wt. (g)	Type	Description	Identification marks	References
Witney, Oxon. (Wi)										
1.	SP352092	?	(187.3)	(69.8)	(31.8)	?	F	Thin rounded butt, oval cross section, rounded edge, two intrusive flaws, pearly grey.		O'Neil, 1966, 162
Woodstock, Oxon. (Wo)										
1.	c. SP44 16	?	?	?	?	?	F	"Neolithic flint chipped celt."		Manning & Leeds, 1920/1, 261
Wilson Collection										
1.	c. SP38 19	BM	38.5	15.0	4.0	–	G	L/s arrowhead from face fragment, creamy white patina, striae.	1910:11-4: 112	Wilson, 1910
2.	c. SP38 19	BM	79.5	50.0	18.0	–	F	Tapered butt, grey, pointed oval cross section.	1910:11-4: 205.	
3.	c. SP38 19	BM	92.0	45.5	20.0	86	F	Thick butt, irregular oval cross section, depression in one face, bluish grey, patches of cortex.	1910:11-4: 210	
4.	c. SP38 19	BM	25.0	20.0	7.0	–	G	Face fragment from near edge, creamy white patina, stained.	1910:11-4: 400	

No.	Grid ref	Mus.					Cond.	Description	Reference
5.	c. SP38 19	BM	33.0	25.5	14.0	–	G	Scraper from face fragment, battered on unground face, stained.	1910:11-4: 401
6.	c. SP38 19	BM	43.0	25.0	6.0 (twisted)	–	G	Face/side fragment, yellowish grey.	1910:11-4: 402
7.	c. SP38 19	BM	52.0	37.0	9.5	–	G	Face fragment, hinge fracture, mottled yellow.	1910:11-4: 403
8.	c. SP38 19	BM	98.0	56.0	29.0	157	F	Tapered thin butt, pointed oval cross section, straight edge, bluish grey, iron staining on ridges.	1910:11-4: 451

Batheaston, Soms. (Bt)

No.	Grid ref	Mus.					Cond.	Description	Reference
1.	c. ST764695	KSM	14.9	19.8	2.9	–	G	Face fragment, white patina, striae.	Ch. Dn. 20 iii 49
2.	c. ST769680	AM	25.0	24.0	12.0	–	G	Thin butt, oval cross section, flattened on one side, striae, heavy white patina.	1927:6032a
3.	c. ST769680	AM	20.0	21.0	4.0	–	G	Face fragment, heavy white patina, striae.	1927:6032b
4.	c. ST756704	?	?	?	?	–	G	"...several polished axe fragments....".	O. S. Ant. No. ST77 SE11

Charlcombe, Soms. (Co)

No.	Grid ref	Mus.					Cond.	Description	Reference
1.	c. ST726692	?	?	?	?	?	F	"...an unpolished flint axe....".	O. S. Ant. No. ST76 NW13

No.	National Grid Reference of findspot	Present location	Max. dimensions (mm) Length	width	thickness	Wt. (g)	Type	Description	Identification marks	References
Charlcombe, Soms. (Co)										
2.	c. ST732678	?	?	?	?	–	G	"The middle cut of a large polished flint celt....".		O.S. Ant. No. ST76 NW35
3.	c. ST723688	AM	30.0	52.0	9.0	–	G	Face fragment, heavy white patina, slight staining.	1958:472	
4.	ST726696	KSM	31.5	28.2	4.4	–	G	Edge fragment, grey patina, striae.	F 123 (LL2, 31043)	
5.	ST726694	KSM	13.6 (curved)	42.9	10.4	–	G	Edge fragment, grey patina, striae.	F 125 (2636, LL)	
6.	ST721695	KSM	57.4	63.0	30.0	–	G	Crude scraper from body fragment, grey, off-white patina, slight staining.	F 572 (Slates, 11747)	
7.	ST726694	KSM	24.2	14.5	7.2	–	G	Face fragment, white patina, some staining, striae.	F 643	
8.	ST726694	KSM	27.0	33.2	6.5	–	G	Face fragment, white patina, some staining, striae.	F 1022 (77)	
9.	ST721695	KSM	37.8	27.8	17.5	–	G	Face fragment, light grey patina, striae, fire damaged.	F 1302 (Slates)	

10.	ST726694	56.1	31.8	9.4	–	G	Face fragment, mottled grey, some iron staining, striae, fire damaged. F 1304 (LL, 6238)
11.	ST726694	29.3	22.7	6.5	–	G	Side/face fragment, white patina, some staining, striae, flattened side. F 1305 (LL)
12.	ST726694	31.3	31.6	10.5	–	G	Face fragment, mottled grey, some staining, striae, polished area. F 1306 (LL, 281237)
13.	ST726694	39.1	35.7	7.5	–	G	Face fragment, white patina, some staining, striae. F 1308 (LL, 231032)
14.	ST726694	20.2	15.0	2.3	–	G	Face fragment, greyish patina, some staining, striae. F 1316 (LL)
15.	ST726694	27.3	21.7	4.1	–	G	Face fragment, from near edge, creamy patina, some staining, striae. F 1317 (LL, 6332)
16.	ST721695	23.6	29.9	7.2	–	G	Face fragment, white patina, striae, staining. F 1318 (Slates)
17.	ST737685	33.9	15.8	3.3 (curved)	–	G	Face fragment, white/grey patina, slight staining, striae. F 1320 (ULF3, 5846)
18.	ST735685	24.8	23.0	4.2	–	G	Face fragment, light greyish patina, striae. F 1808 (ULF2, 2646)

No.	National Grid Reference of findspot	Present location	Max. dimensions (mm) Length	width	thickness	Wt. (g)	Type	Description	Identification marks	References
Charlcombe, Soms. (Co)										
19.	ST735685	KSM	9.9	16.9	2.4	–	G	Face fragment, whitish patina, striae.	F 1909 (ULF2)	Dobson, 1931, 243
Kelston, Soms. (Kl)										
1.	ST70 67	?	?	?	?	–	G	"Fragment of polished flint....".		
St. Catherine, Soms. (St. C)										
1.	ST772695	KSM	20.1	15.8	2.0	–	G	Face fragment, white patina, stained, striae.	HD	
Barton-on-the-Heath, Warks. (BOH)										
1.	SP25 32	WCM	140.0	58.0	38.0	(383)	G	Thin butt, oval cross section, rounded sides, heavy mottled buff patina, trace iron stain, sides and part of faces battered and constricted where hafted.	Bloxam Coll. 57	Clinch, 1904, 216; O.S. Ant. No. SP23 SE3
Ashton Keynes, Wilts. (AK)										
1.	SU050951	KB	(119.0)	(45.0)	?	–	G	"Body fragment, yellow flint."		Anon., 1973, 127

Box, Wilts. (Bx)

1.	c. ST835683	DM	30.4	13.3	10.4	–	G	Face/side fragment, heavy white patina, some staining, striae.	54-1967 Shaw Mellor Coll.
2.	c. ST843679	DM	39.8	61.8	16.7	–	G	Almost complete edge, white patina, some staining, striae.	54-1967 Shaw Mellor Coll.
3.	c. ST808695	DM	44.4	22.2	15.6	–	G	Corner fragment, white patina, some staining, striae.	54-1967 Shaw Mellor Coll.
4.	c. ST814690	DM	35.9	41.8	21.4	–	G	Body fragment from near butt, white patina, some iron stain, striae.	54-1967 Shaw Mellor Coll.
5.	c. ST814690	DM	36.5	24.3	10.0 (curved)	–	G	Face fragment, white patina, some iron staining, striae, battered one end.	54-1967 Shaw Mellor Coll.
6.	c. ST816694	DM	28.8	29.2	13.2	–	G	Face fragment, white patina, some staining, striae.	54-1967 Shaw Mellor Coll.
7.	c. ST816694	DM	39.5	8.8	14.6	–	G	Side fragment from near corner, white patina, some staining, striae.	54-1967 Shaw Mellor Coll.
8.	c. ST816674	?	?	?	?	?	G&F	"...a rechipped polished flint axe....".	Grinsell, 1957, 44

No.	National Grid Reference of findspot	Present location	Max. dimensions (mm) Length	width	thickness	Wt. (g)	Type	Description	Identification marks	References
Box, Wilts. (Bx)										
9.	c. ST817675	KSM	61.5	30.0	13.5	—	G & F	Thin butt, white patina, some staining, small area of striae.	F 543 (KD1, 28648)	
10.	ST817675	KSM	23.4	30.5	6.7	—	G	Face fragment, white patina, slight staining, striae, polished.	F 1023 (KD1c, 31346)	
11.	ST817675	KSM	21.3	32.1	6.5	—	G	Face fragment, white patina, slight staining, striae, polished.	F 2244 (KD1c, 1011≤6)	
12.	ST817675	KSM	45.8	35.4	20.0	—	G	Body fragment from near butt, oval cross section, rounded sides, white patina, some staining, striae.	F 573 (KD2, 41134)	
13.	ST817673	KSM	27.0	23.6	4.5	—	G	Face fragment, greyish patina, striae.	F 1315 (KD4)	
Chippenham, Wilts. (Cp)										
1.	c. ST91 73	AM	180.0	65.0	40.0	505	F	Thin butt, irregular lozenge cross section, grey.	1955-214e Passmore Coll.	O.S. Ant. No. ST97 SW23

Colerne, Wilts. (Cn)

#	Location	Coll.	L	W	T	?	Cond.	Description	Reference
1.	c. ST820730	DM	72.3	56.0	30.7	–	G	Core from face fragment, white patina, some staining, striae, secondary retouch.	LUC 8; 50-1968 Shaw Mellor Coll.
2.	c. ST818740	DM	43.5	40.6	18.1	–	G	Edge fragment, sides flaked, white patina, some staining, striae.	BWC 1512; 50-1968 Shaw Mellor Coll.
3.	c. ST818740	DM	58.7	44.0	22.3	–	G	Core from fragment, white patina, slight staining, striae, small polished area.	BWC 452; 50-1968 Shaw Mellor Coll.
4.	c. ST818740	DM	124.0	66.1	35.4	–	G	Body fragment, butt missing, oval cross section, flattened sides, grey, white patina, slight staining, striae.	BWC 1514; 50-1968 Shaw Mellor Coll.
5.	c. ST818740	DM	64.1	53.8	30.3	–	G	Thin butt, white patina, some staining, striae.	BWC 451; 50-1968 Shaw Mellor Coll.
6.	c. ST81 71	?	?	?	?	?	G	"Polished flint axe...."	Grinsell, 1957, 59
7.	ST797699	KSM	31.5	23.3	14.8	–	G	Corner fragment, flattened side, white patina, slight staining, striae.	F 1301 (Banner Down, 18632)

National Grid Reference of findspot	Present location	Max. dimensions (mm) Length	width	thickness	Wt. (g)	Type	Description	Identification marks	References
Colerne, Wilts. (Cn)									
8. ST797699	KSM	45.3	47.0	21.1	–	G	Body fragment from which flakes were struck, rounded sides, white patina, slight staining, striae.	F 577 (Banner Down, 311233)	
Corsham, Wilts. (Co)									
1. c. ST860718	DM	76.8	60.6	35.8	–	G & F	Thin butt, reflaked, striae on sides, heavy white patina, some staining.	54-1967 Shaw Mellor Coll.	
2. c. ST861682	DM	58.9	44.4	17.9	–	G	Body fragment from near butt, white patina, some iron staining, striae.	54-1967 Shaw Mellor Coll.	
Crudwell, Wilts. (Cu)									
1. c. ST95 93	DM	225.0	69.5	36.7	(737)	G	Thin butt, oval cross section, flattened sides, mottled brown patina, patches of cortex, inclusion, striae, polished.	DM 1480	Evans, 1897, 111
2. c. ST95 93	DM	238.0	74.2	38.3	(822)	G	Thin butt, oval cross section, flattened sides, grey, mottled brown patina, striae, polished.	DM 1482	O. S. Ant. No. ST99 SE6

No.	Grid ref.							Description	Reference
3.	c. ST95 93	?	?	?	?	?	G	"...the third was broken, but was much of the same character and size....".	Anon., 1863, 149
4.	c. ST94 92	AW	25.3	23.2	5.3 (curved)	–	G	Corner fragment, white patina, little staining, striae, polished edge.	17

Monkton Farleigh, Wilts. (MF)

No.	Grid ref.							Description	Reference
1.	c. ST805655	DM	48.6	32.8	15.1	–	G	Body fragment from near butt, white patina, slight staining.	54-1967 Shaw Mellor Coll.
2.	c. ST805655	DM	53.2	35.5	21.9	–	G	Face/side fragment from near butt, one face has a flatter profile than the other, white patina, some staining, striae.	54-1967 Shaw Mellor Coll.
3.	c. ST805655	DM	22.7	15.4	2.7	–	G	Face fragment, white patina, slight staining, striae.	54-1967 Shaw Mellor Coll.
4.	c. ST805655	DM	30.4	23.4	13.6	–	G	Thin butt, white patina, some staining, striae on sides, fire damaged.	54-1967 Shaw Mellor Coll.
5.	c. ST805655	DM	36.7	53.0	16.6	–	G	Damaged edge fragment, evidence of regrinding, white patina, some iron stain, striae.	54-1967 Shaw Mellor Coll.

No.	National Grid Reference of findspot	Present location	Max. dimensions (mm) Length	width	thickness	Wt. (g)	Type	Description	Identification marks	References
Monkton Farleigh, Wilts. (MF)										
6.	c. ST805655	DM	79.2	46.0	22.3	–	G	Thin butt reground at a steep angle at the break, white patina, some staining, striae.	54-1967 Shaw Mellor Coll.	
7.	ST797658	KSM	23.5	31.3	15.7	–	G	Thin butt, oval cross section, white patina, some staining.	F 583 (FD,18932)	Grinsell,1957,90
8.	ST797658	KSM	33.8	15.5	3.9	–	G	Face fragment with change of angle to side, area of cortex, white patina, some staining, striae.	F 1314 (FD,2732)	Dobson,1931,247
9.	ST797658	KSM	17.0	15.8	21.0	–	G	Flattened side fragment, white patina, some staining, striae.	F 1309 (FD2,20832)	
10.	ST806637	?	?	?	?	?	?	"Flint axes..believed destroyed during blitz on Bath, 1941."		Grinsell,1957,90
11.	ST801664	KSM	30.0	16.5	6.5	–	G	Small tapered 'chisel' from edge fragment, striae are at right angles to long axis, white patina, some staining.	F 130 (SL,22434)	

No.	Site	Mus.	L	W	T	?	Cond.	Description	Find
12.	ST801664	KSM	27.9	21.1	8.0 (curved)	–	G	Face fragment, fine retouch on one side, white patina, some staining, striae.	F 1608
13.	ST802664	KSM	62.5	52.3	30.0	–	G	Thin butt, oval cross section, rounded sides, white patina, some staining, striae.	F 71 (S2, 81032)
14.	ST802664	KSM	44.7	16.9	8.4	–	G	'Chisel' from edge fragment, striae are at right angles to long axis, white patina.	F 127 (S2, 28434)
15.	ST802664	KSM	38.2	16.7	5.3	–	G	'Chisel' from edge fragment, striae at right angles to long axis, white patina, some staining.	F 129 (S2, 41232)
16.	ST802664	KSM	32.8	14.0	6.5	–	G	Small tapered 'chisel' from edge fragment, striae at right angles to long axis, white patina, some staining.	F 132 (S2, 1532)
17.	ST802664	KSM	23.7	13.7	4.2	–	G	Face fragment, white patina, some staining, striae. (S2)	F 134
18.	ST802664	KSM	27.0	21.8	5.5	–	G	Face fragment, grey/brown, creamy patina, striae. (S2/SWW)	F 1313
19.	ST802664	KSM	18.3	20.7	3.0	–	G	Edge fragment, white patina, some staining, striae. (S2, 301032)	F 1319

No.	National Grid Reference of findspot	Present location	Max. dimensions (mm) Length	width	thickness	Wt. (g)	Type	Description	Identification marks	References
Monkton Farleigh, Wilts. (MF)										
20.	ST802664	KSM	21.7	17.3	3.8 (curved)	–	G	Face fragment, white patina, striae.	F 1812 (S2, 26433)	
21.	ST804664	KSM	22.7	55.6	28.5	–	G	Body fragment, oval cross section, rounded sides, white patina, some staining, striae.	F 124 (S3, 8434)	
22.	ST804664	KSM	36.9	16.4	6.0	–	G	End scraper from face fragment, white patina, some staining, striae.	F 131 (S3, 16634)	
23.	ST804664	KSM	24.1	25.3	5.7	–	G	Face fragment, white patina, some staining, striae.	F 1307 (S3)	
24.	ST802662	KSM	30.0	27.4	17.4	–	G	Side/face fragment from near edge, creamy/white patina, some staining, striae.	F 1303 (S5)	
25.	c. ST796655	?	?	?	?	–	F	"...an unpolished butt-end of a flint axe....".		O. S. Ant. No. ST76 NE35
26.	c. ST801663	?	?	?	?	?	G	"Ground flint axe....".		Grinsell, 1957, 90

Winsley, Wilts. (Ws)

1.	c. ST792624	DM	40.0	45.7	19.8	–	G	Edge fragment, white patina, some staining, striae.	Wins 1	Collins, 1912, 380
2.	c. ST792624	DM	26.5	20.0	3.6	–	G	Face fragment, white patina, slight staining, striae.	Wins 1	Underwood, 1945/7, 441
3.	c. ST792624	DM	50.6	48.2	19.8	–	G	Body fragment, white patina on part of side, some staining, striae.	Wins 1	Grinsell, 1957, 124

Cotswolds (Cots)

1.	?	GCM	105.0	54.6	26.7	146	G & F	Adze from edge fragment, oval cross section, mottled grey.	A 3423	
2.	Charlton	CAGM	39.5	45.5	20.3	–	G	Thin butt, flattened sides, mottled grey/brown, white patina, striae.	4. 1933-100 Cardew Coll.	
3.	?	CAGM	41.9	47.0	27.5	–	G	Thin butt, flattened sides, mottled, white patina, striae.	6. 1933-100 Cardew Coll.	
4.	?	CAGM	34.5	29.5	16.7	–	G	Body fragment, oval cross section, flattened sides, dark grey, white patina, some iron stain, striae.	7. 1933-100 Cardew Coll.	

No.	National Grid Reference of findspot	Present location	Max. diameter (mm) Length	width	thickness	Wt. (g)	Type	Description	Identification marks	References
Cotswolds (Cots)										
5.	?	CAGM	40.0	46.4	24.5	–	G	Thin butt, slightly flattened sides, mottled creamy patina.	8. 1933-100	Cardew Coll.
6.	?	CAGM	17.1	45.0	14.7	–	G	Corner/edge fragment, heavy white patina, some staining, striae, polished on one face.	9. 1933-100	Cardew Coll.
7.	?	CAGM	37.4	36.0	13.0	–	G	Edge fragment, heavy white patina, some staining, striae, polished on one face.	10. 1933-100	Cardew Coll.
8.	?	CAGM	43.5	37.0	24.0	–	G	Body fragment from near butt, heavy cream patina, staining, striae.	11. 1933-100	Cardew Coll.
9.	?	CAGM	53.0	16.0	22.0	–	G	Edge fragment, light grey, heavy white patina, some staining, striae, polished on one face.	12. 1933-100	Cardew Coll.
10.	?	CAGM	18.7	31.2	7.4	–	G	Face fragment, heavy white patina, some staining.	13. 1933-100	Cardew Coll.

No.	Location	Museum						Description	Ref.
11.	?	CAGM	33.9	29.0	11.0 (curved)	–	G	Corner fragment, heavy white patina, some staining, striae.	14. 1933-100 Cardew Coll.
12.	?	CAGM	47.4	43.7	27.5	–	G	Body fragment, flattened side, heavy patina, some staining, striae.	15. 1933-100 Cardew Coll.
13.	?	CAGM	45.4	22.5	16.5	–	G	Battered edge fragment, mottled grey/brown, heavy patina, striae.	16. 1933-100 Cardew Coll.
14.	?	CAGM	17.3	34.5	12.0	–	G	Edge fragment, heavy white patina, some staining, striae.	17. 1933-100 Cardew Coll.
15.	?	CAGM	56.0	38.5	19.4	–	G	Face/edge fragment, traces of sides, mottled grey, fire damaged, striae.	18. 1933-100 Cardew Coll.
16.	?	CAGM	32.0	38.5	19.3	–	G	Face fragment, mottled grey, fire damaged, striae.	19. 1933-100 Cardew Coll.
17.	?	CAGM	34.8	22.5	17.9	–	G	Flattened side fragment, grey, white patina, some staining, striae.	82. 1913-76 Wild Coll.
18.	Brockhampton ?	CAGM	37.0	40.7	16.3	–	G	Face/side fragment, creamy patina, some staining, striae.	Bro
19.	Calcot ?	SM	62.3	41.0	9.9	–	G	Scraper from face fragment, pronounced curvature, heavy white patina.	Ct

No.	National Grid Reference of findspot	Present location	Max. dimensions (mm) Length	width	thickness	Wt. (g)	Type	Description	Identification marks	References
Cotswolds (Cots)										
20.	?	CAGM	31.9	12.8	3.7	–	G	Face fragment, light grey, light patina, trace staining, striae.	Magd.1e	Gracie, 1970, 9
21.	?	CAGM	37.0	33.0	5.9 (curved)	–	G	Corner fragment, mottled, white patina, some staining, striae, polished.	9	
22.	?	CAGM	18.2	50.0	22.5	–	F	Body fragment, oval cross section, mottled grey, heavy white patina, slight staining, fire damaged.	51	

BIBLIOGRAPHY

Abbreviations used in the bibliography are in accordance with those recommended by the Council for British Archaeology in their Standard List of Abbreviated Titles of Current Periodicals (Edition of November 1973).

Adkins, R. (1974). Neolithic Flint and Stone Axes from the Middle Thames. (Undergraduate Thesis presented to the Dept. of Archaeology, University College, Cardiff).

Anon., (1863). Proceedings of the Association, April 22. J. British Archaeol. Assoc., XIX, 148-150.

(1881). Proceedings of the Association, Wednesday, June 1. J. British Archaeol. Assoc., XXXVII, 213-219.

(1973). Wiltshire Archaeological Register for 1972. Wiltshire Archaeol. Natur. Hist. Mag., LXVIII (B), 126-139.

Atkinson, R. J. C. (1947). A Middle Bronze Age Barrow at Cassington, Oxon. Oxoniensia, XI/XII, 5-26.

(1948). Archaeological Notes. Oxoniensia, XIII, 66-67.

Bloxam, M. H. (---). Fragmenta Sepulchralia. N.B. This fragment, printed in 1840-50 by T. Combe at Oxford University Presss, was never published.

Bradley, R. (1972/3). Prehistorians and Pastoralists in Neolithic and Bronze Age England. World Archaeol., IV, 192-204.

Brown, K. (1973). Personal communication.

Brown, P. D. C. (1968). Archaeological Notes. Oxoniensia, XXXIII, 137-138.

Bruce-Mitford, R. L. S. (1938). A Hoard of Neolithic Axes from Peaslake, Surrey. Antiq. J., XVIII, 279-284.

Buckman, S. S. (1903). The Cotteswold Hills: A Geographical Enquiry. Proc. Cotteswold Natur. Fld. Club, XIV, 205-242.

Bunch, B. & Fell, C. I. (1949). A Stone-Axe Factory at Pike of Stickle, Great Langdale, Westmorland. Proc. Prehist. Soc., XV, 1-20.

Burchard, A. (1973). A Waisted Flint Axe from Corsley. Wiltshire Archaeol. Natur. Hist. Mag., LXVIII (B), 118-119.

Burton, R. J. (1929). Archaeology of Bisley Hundred. Trans. Bristol Gloucestershire Archaeol. Soc., LI, 253-260.

Cardew, J. H. (1890/1). The Surface Flint Implements of the Cotteswold Hills. Trans. Bristol Gloucestershire Archaeol. Soc., XV, 246-253.

Case, H. J. (1957). Archaeological Notes. Oxoniensia, XXII, 104-106.

(1963). Notes on the Finds and on Ring Ditches in the Oxford Region. Oxoniensia, XXVIII, 19-52.

Clifford, E. M., Garrod, D. A. E. & Gracie, H. S. (1954). Flint Implements from Gloucestershire. Antiq. J., XXXIV, 178-187.

Clinch, G. (1904). The Victoria History of the Counties of England: Warwickshire I.

Collins, W. G. (1912). A Prehistoric Site at Conkwell near Bradford-on-Avon. The Antiquary, XLVIII, 380-389.

Cowper, H. (1863). Celt of Light Coloured Flint Found at Panshanger, Hertfordshire. Archaeol. J., XX, 192-193.

Crawford, O. G. S. (1925). Long Barrows of the Cotswolds.

Curwen, E. (1929). Hoard of Celts from Sussex. Antiq. J., IX, 42-43.

Dillon, H. (1875). On Flint Implements, etc. Found in the Neighbourhood of Ditchley, Oxon. J. Anthropol. Inst. Gr. Brit. Ir., V, 33-35.

Dixon, P. (1972). Personal communication.

Dobson, D. P. (1931). Archaeology of Somerset.

Edmunds, F. H. & Oakley, K. P. (1958). Central England District: British Regional Geology.

Evans, J. (1897). Ancient Stone Implements of Great Britain. (2nd edition).

Fowler, P. J. & Miles, H. (eds.) (1972). Excavation, Fieldwork and Finds. Archaeol. Rev. (CBA Groups 12,13), VII, 12-65.

Gettins, G. L., Taylor, H. & Grinsell, L. V. (1953). The Marshfield Barrows. Trans. Bristol Gloucestershire Archaeol. Soc., LXXII, 23-44.

Gracie, H. S. (1970). Mesolithic Gloucester. Trans. Bristol Gloucestershire Archaeol. Soc., LXXXIX, 6-12.

Gray, J. W. (1911). The North and Mid Cotteswolds and the Vale of Moreton during the Glacial Epoch. Proc. Cotteswold Natur. Fld. Club, XVII, 257-274.

(1912/3). Notes on the North and Mid Cotteswold Flints. Proc. Cheltenham Natur. Sci. Soc., II (2), 65-75.

Griffiths, O. (1949/52). Countryside Notes and Queries. Gloucestershire Countryside, VII, 305.

Grimes, W. F. (1939). The Excavation of Ty Isaf Long Cairn, Brecknockshire. Proc. Prehist. Soc., V, 119-142.

Grinsell, L. V. (1957). The Victoria History of the Counties of England: Wiltshire I (i).

(1964). The Royce Collection at Stow-on-the-Wold. Trans. Bristol Gloucestershire Archaeol. Soc., LXXXIII, 5-33.

(1968). City Museum, Bristol: Recent Archaeological Accessions. Bristol Archaeol. Res. Grp. Bull., III (3), 64-65.

Hadfield, C. & Hadfield, A. M. (eds.) (1973). The Cotswolds: A New Study.

Hamlin, A. (1963). Excavation of Ring Ditches at Stanton Harcourt. Oxoniensia, XXVIII, 1-18.

Harrison, E. E. (1968). A Polished Flint Axe from Cobham. Surrey Archaeol. Collect., LXV, 129.

Keef, P. A. M. (1940). Flint Chipping Sites and Hearths on Bedham Hill near Pulborough. Sussex Archaeol. Collect., LXXXI, 215-234.

Kellaway, G. A. & Welch, F. B. A. (1948). Bristol and Gloucester District: British Regional Geology.

Knight, R. J. (1973). Personal communication.

Leeds, E. T. (1938). Four Polished Stone Axes. Oxoniensia, III, 168-169.

Lowther, A. W. G. (1957). Flint Axes from Ewhurst. Surrey Archaeol. Collect., LV, 118.

Lucy, W. C. (1872). The Gravels of the Severn, Avon and Evenlode and their Extension over the Cotteswold Hills. Proc. Cotteswold Natur. Fld. Club. V, 71-142.

(1892). A Slight History of Flint Implements, with especial reference to our own and adjacent areas. Proc. Cotteswold Natur. Fld. Club, X, 22-38.

Lysons, S. (1821). Account of the Remains of a Roman Villa discovered in the Parish of Great Witcombe in the County of Gloucestershire. Archaeologia, XIX, 178-183.

Manby, T. G. (1974). Grooved Ware Sites in Yorkshire and the North of England. British Archaeol. Reports, IX.

Manning, P. & Leeds, E. T. (1920/1). An Archaeological Survey of Oxfordshire. Archaeologia, LXXI, 243-264.

McKenny Hughes, T. (1897). On the evidence bearing upon the early history of man which is derived from the form, condition of surface and mode of occurrence of dressed flints. Archaeol. J., LIV, 363-376.

Needham, S. (1975). Personal communication.

O'Neil, H. E. (1966). A Neolithic Flint Axe from Witney, Oxon. Oxoniensia, XXXI, 162.

Piggott, S. (1962). The West Kennet Long Barrow: Excavations 1955-56.

Pollitt, (1931). Neolithic Hoard from Essex. Antiq. J., XI, 57-58.

Reade, T. M., Buckman, S. S. & Callaway, C. (1903). The Gravel at Moreton-in-Marsh. Proc. Cotteswold Natur. Fld. Club, XIV, 111-118.

Selkirk, A. R. L. (1971). Ascott-under-Wychwood. Curr. Archaeol., III, 7-10.

Semenov, S. A. (1964). Prehistoric Technology.

Sherlock, R. L. (1960). London and Thames Valley: British Regional Geology.

Sieveking, G. de G., Craddock, P. T., Hughes, M. J., Bush, P. & Ferguson, J. (1970). Characterisation of Prehistoric Flint Products. Nature, CCXXVIII, 251-254.

Sieveking, G. de G., Bush, P., Ferguson, J., Craddock, P. T., Hughes, M. J. & Cowell, M. R. (1972). Prehistoric Flint Mines and their Identification as Sources of Raw Material. Archaeometry, XIV (2), 151-176.

Smith, I. F. (1965). Windmill Hill and Avebury: Excavations by Alexander Keiller 1925-1939.

(1968). Report on the Late Neolithic Pits at Cam, Gloucestershire. Trans. Bristol Gloucestershire Archaeol. Soc., LXXXVII, 14-28.

Smith, R. A. (1920/1). Hoards of Neolithic Celts. Archaeologia, LXXI, 113-124.

Sturdy, D. & Sutermeister, H. (1964/5). Archaeological Notes 1962-3. Oxoniensia, XXIX/XXX, 190-193.

Thurnam, J. (1854). Description of a Chambered Tumulus near Uley, Glos. Archaeol. J., XI, 315-327.

Tratman, E. K. (1973). Flint Implements from the Bath Downs: the Collections of J. P. E. Falconer, E. A. Shore and J. W. Gardner. Proc. Univ. Bristol Spelaeol. Soc., XIII (2), 153-169.

Underwood, G. (1945/7). Early British Settlement at Farleigh Wick and Conkwell, Wilts. Wiltshire Archaeol. Natur. Hist. Mag., LI, 440-452.

Wainwright, G. H. & Longworth, I. H. (1971). Durrington Walls: Excavations 1966-68.

Wilson, A. J. (1910). Letter with the collection of flints in the British Museum.

Witchell, A. (1973). Personal communication.

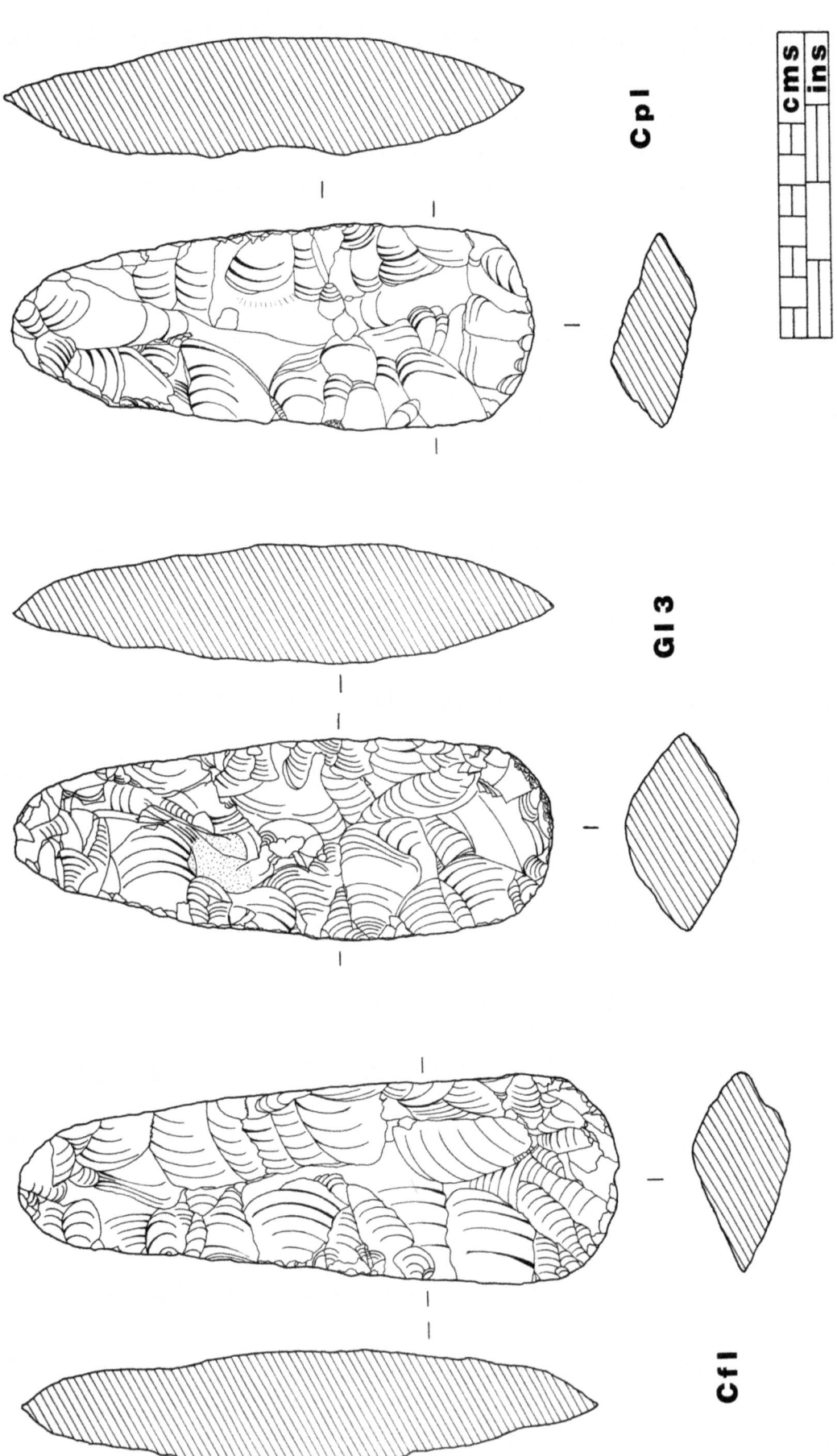

fig 1

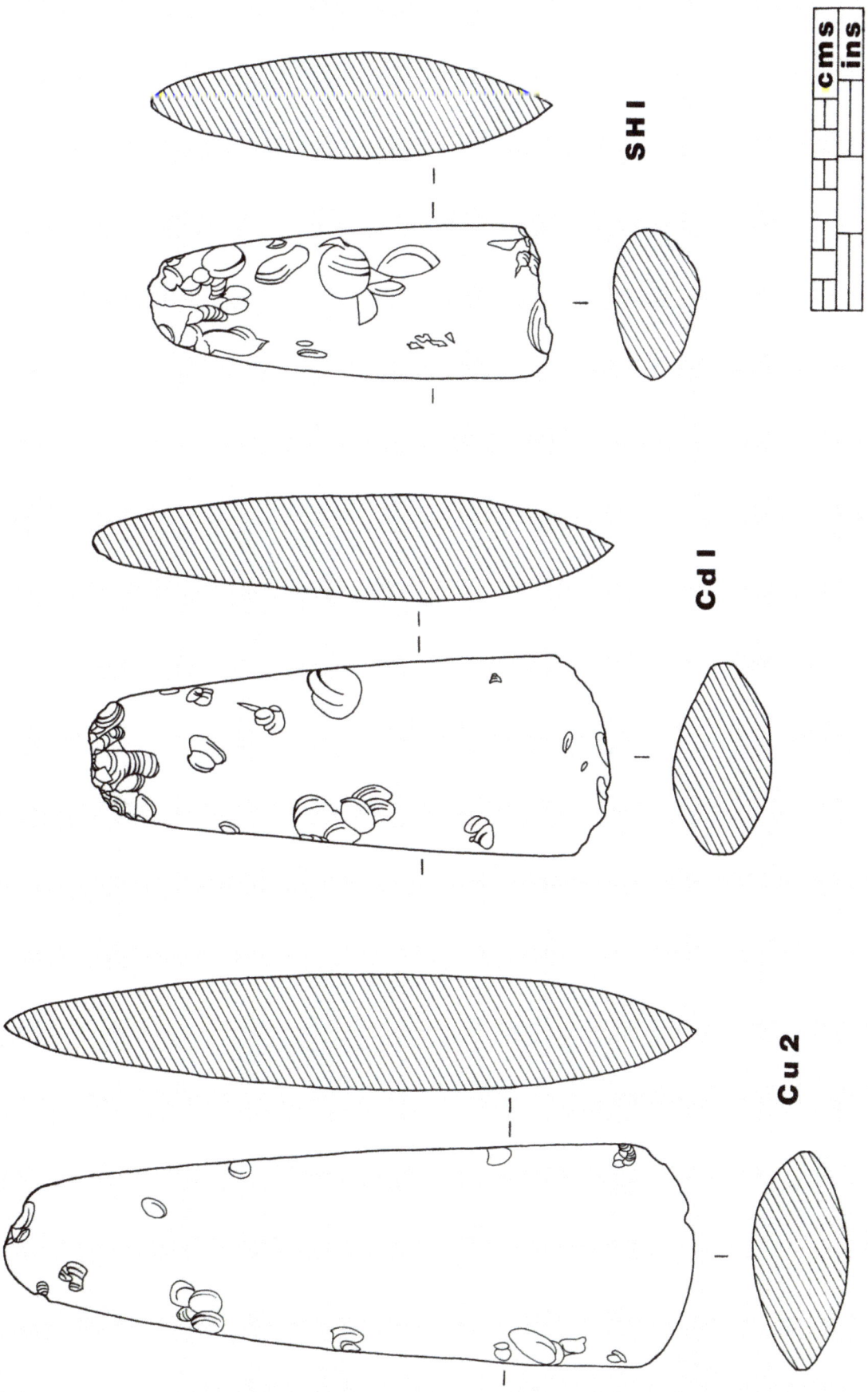

fig 2

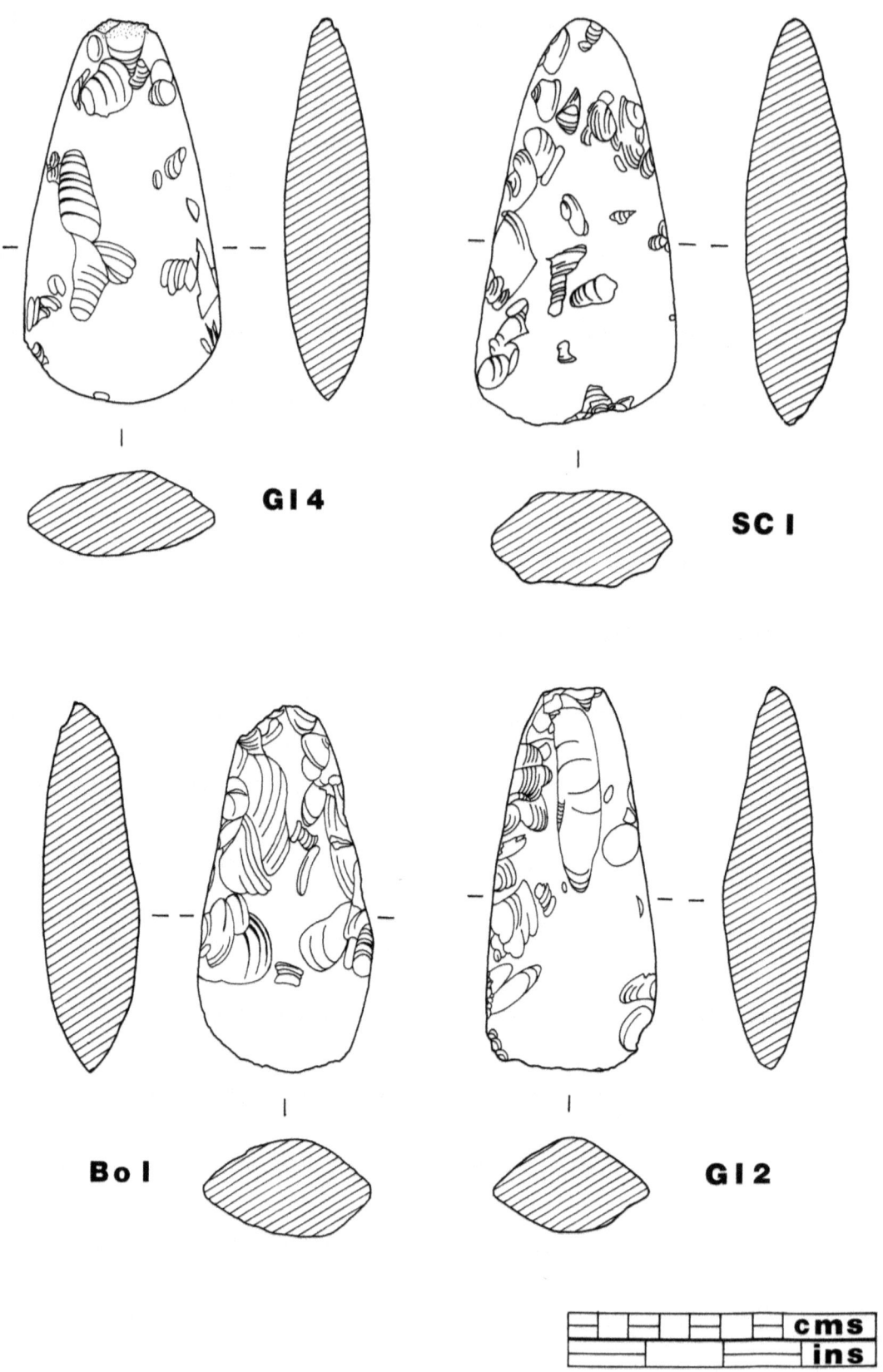

fig 3

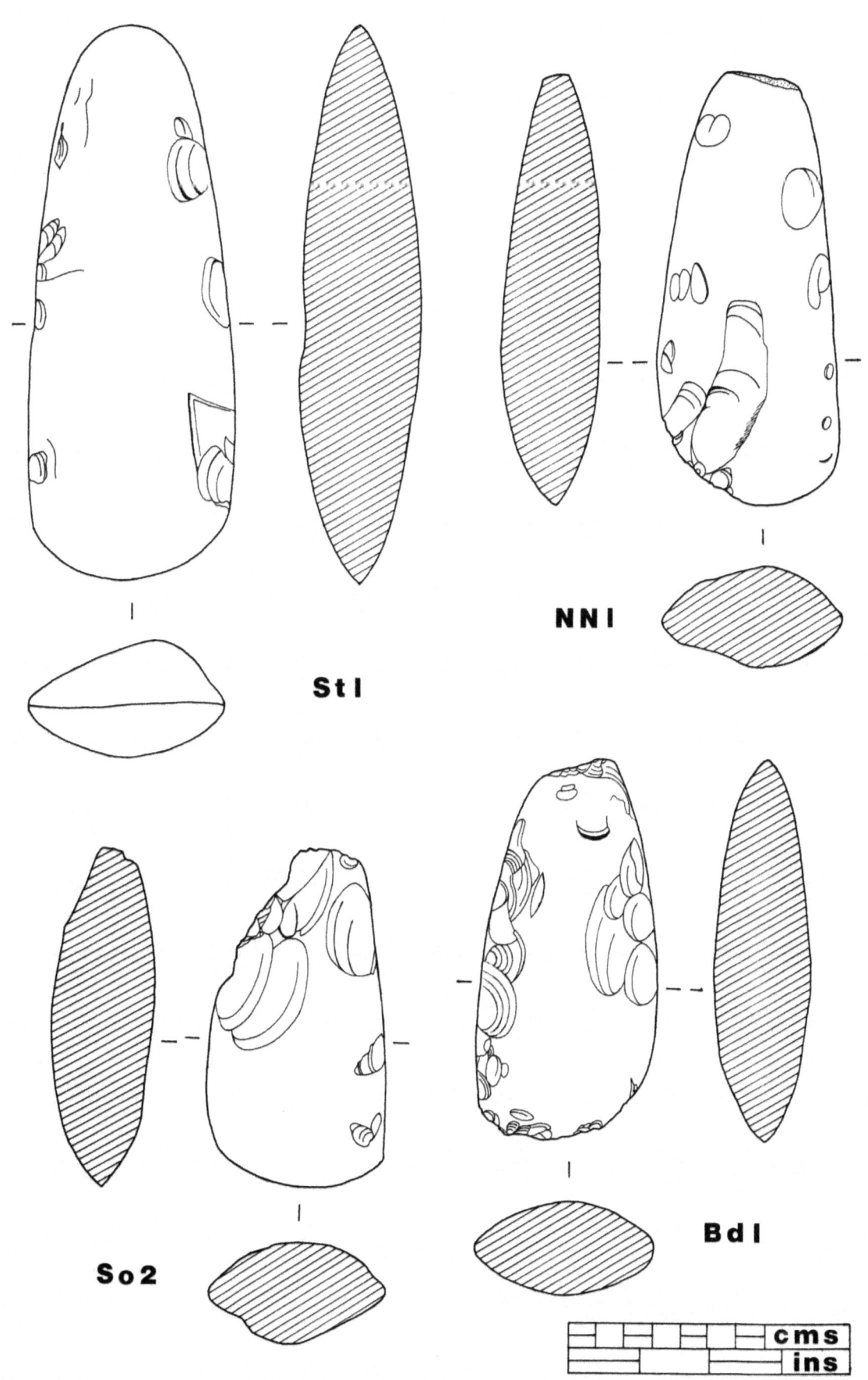

fig 4

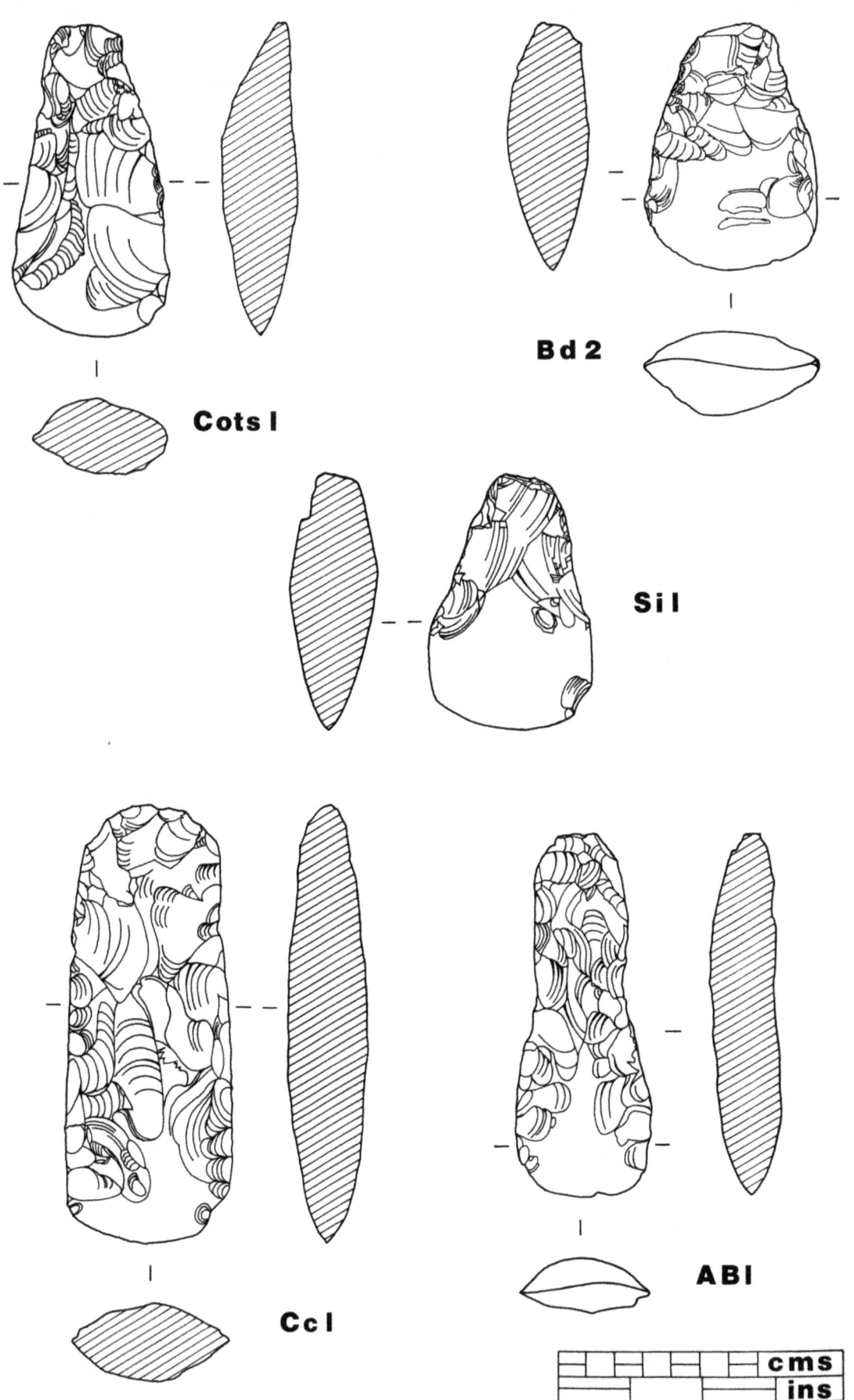

fig 5

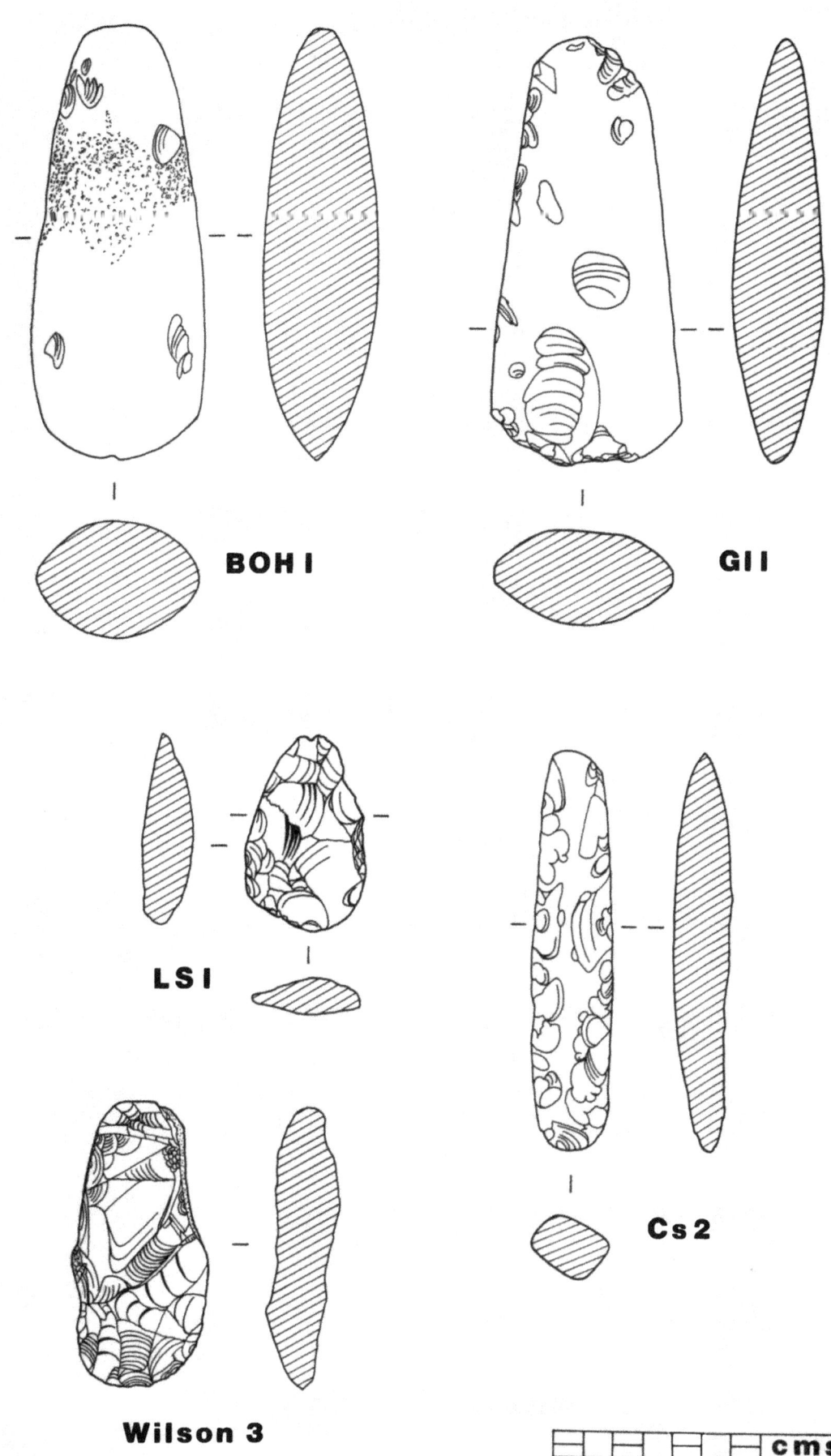

fig 6

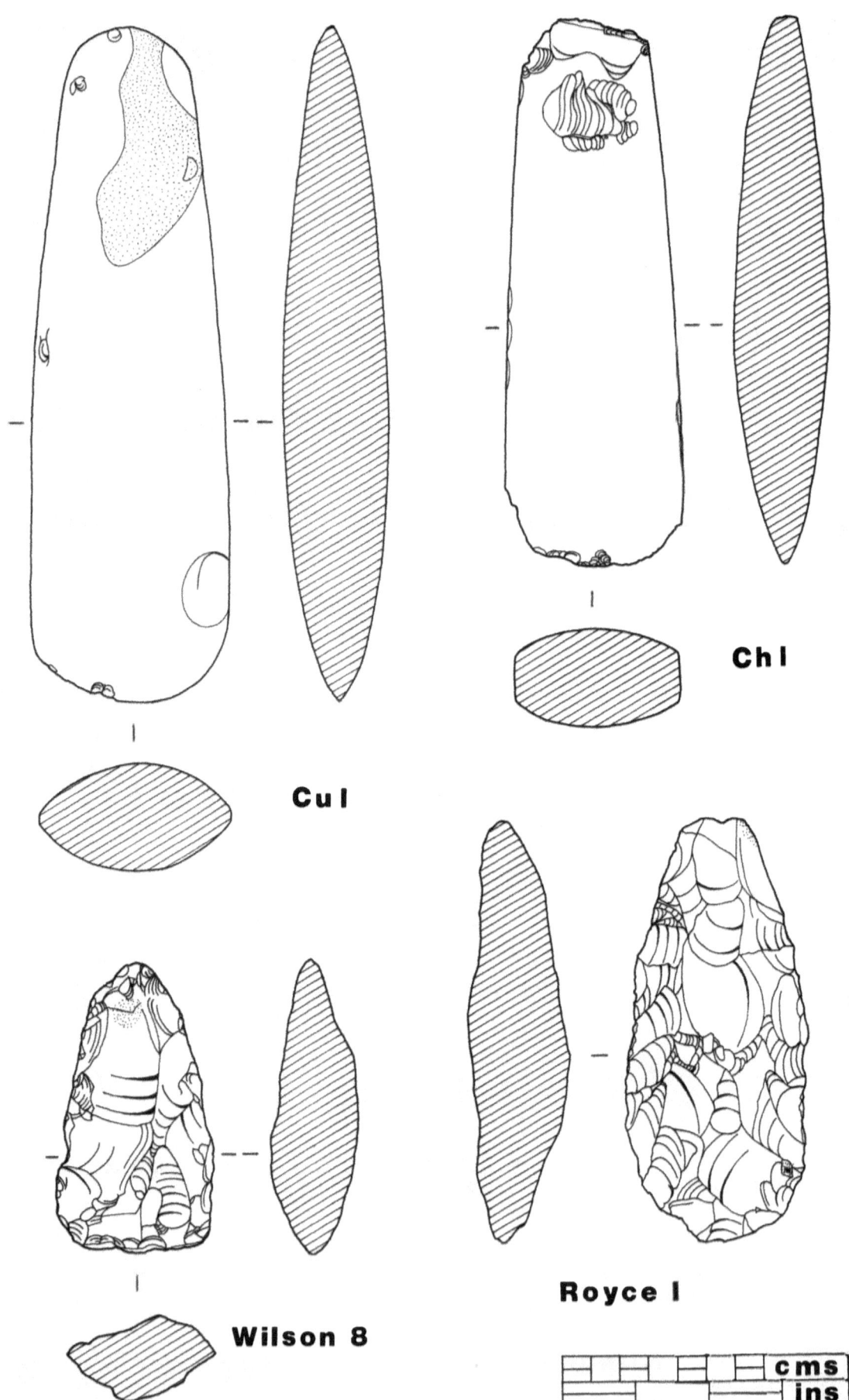

fig 7

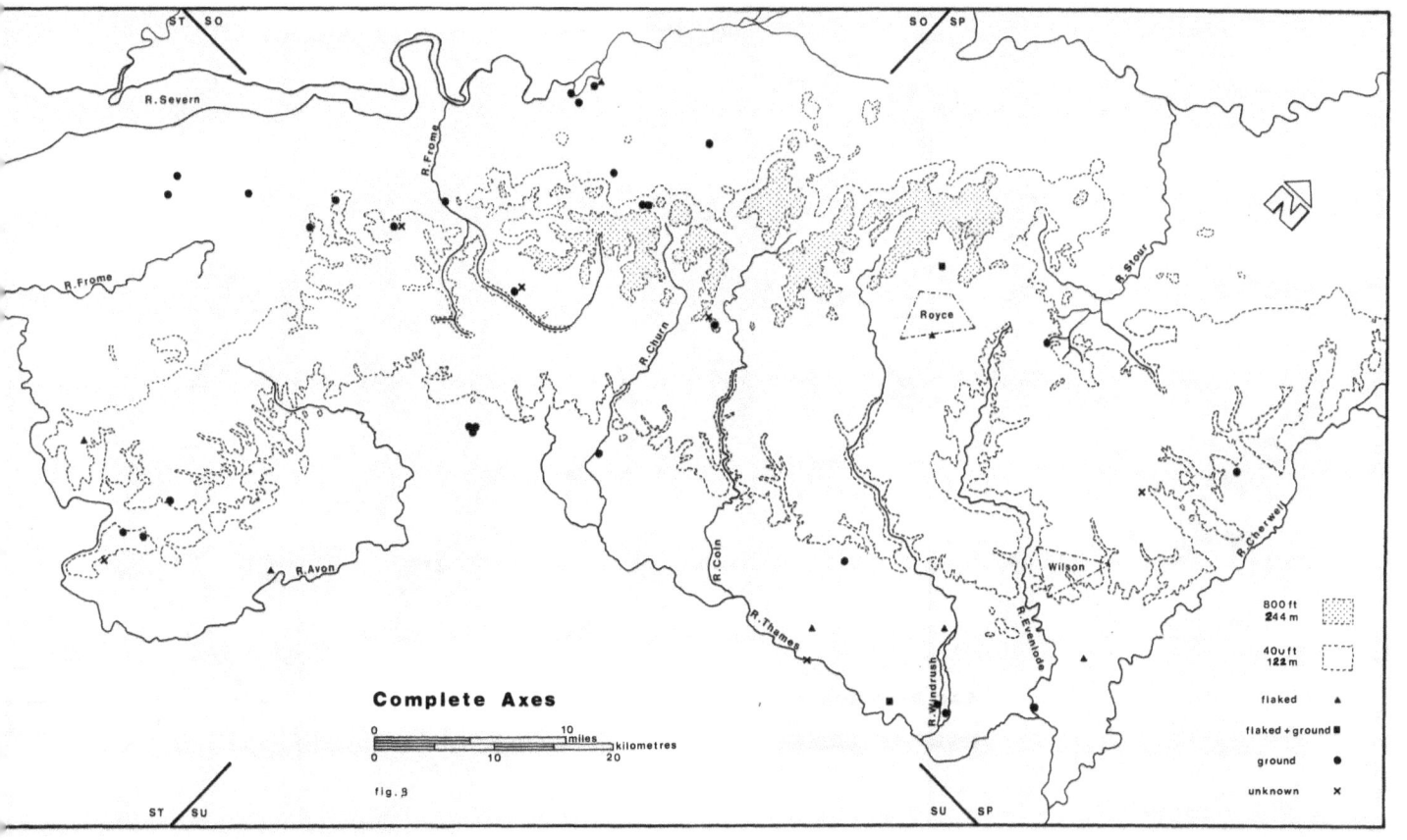

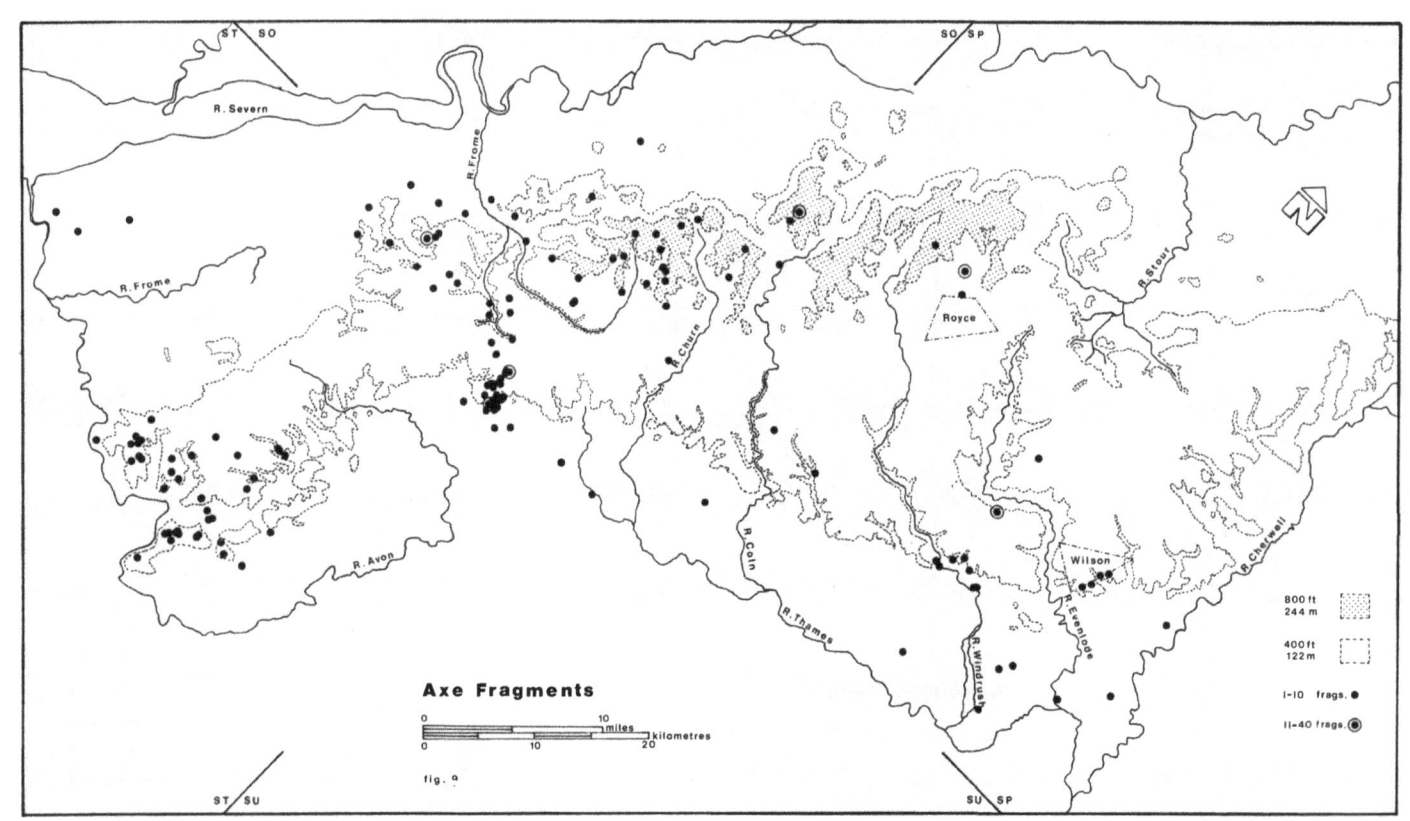

fig. 9 Axe Fragments

www.ingramcontent.com/pod-product-compliance
Lightning Source LLC
Chambersburg PA
CBHW061547010526
44114CB00027B/2952